Praise for
Your Treasured Marriage

"One of the questions that I have when asked to write a book endorsement is this: Is this person writing from "head knowledge" or heart knowledge?" Many years ago, a very wise woman said to me after graduation "Dave, God will give you a life's message. Over the last nearly 50 years I have met, counseled, and shared life with thousands of individuals who have become part of my life's message. One person at the very top of my list is Jeanne Gormick.

We have been friends and coworkers for more than 30 years. During that time, I have watched her struggle with a challenging set of circumstances such as marriage, employment, child rearing, and even death itself. She reminds me of the commercial about the energizer bunny … just keeps going.

Yes, her heart is truly there on every page of this book."

David M Gutknecht, Licensed Professional Counselor

"After reading this book I was most impressed by Ms. Gormick's openness and honesty in sharing her journey to an authentic faith found in Jesus Christ and the impact this had on her marriage. She shares her lifelong pursuit for a 'Treasured' marriage, which includes their struggles through a variety of life's problems and joys. This journey took her through a variety of faith expressions including Unitarianism, Judaism, and finally to becoming a follower of

"Messiah" Jesus. She shares openly about living with an unbelieving husband and her struggles of being a highly motivated, self-sufficient woman who ultimately learns the importance of submitting to the guidance and direction from the Lord Jesus Christ and his Word. Her insights on marriage are spot on, her stories are inspiring, her struggles are real and her faith is authentic. I highly recommend this book to all who desire to build a marriage that is 'Treasured'."

Retired Pastor Bruce Erickson, Life Bible Fellowship Church

"In reading *Your Treasured Marriage,* we are all gently encouraged to dig a little deeper to find the hidden treasure in our own difficult life situations. Jeanne's circumstances are personally relatable, and cause us to marvel at the number of simultaneously occurring difficult scenarios she was able to successfully walk through. Her life-story is an inspiration and testimony of the inner-strength given by God to be resilient and committed to loving at all times and in all circumstances."

Katy Jean Marzolf, Best-Selling Author of *The One Body of Christ*

"A great book about compromise and communication as a way to keep a marriage strong through the power of Jesus.

A must-read for engaged couples ready to marry and for already married couples who are planning on having children or are struggling through parts of their marriage. Or for people just like me who plan on being married again someday and want to get it right this time!

God is Love; therefore, He has to be made the most important part of any relationship that's going to last!"

Lori Kuznicki, Hospice Staffing Coordinator

"Jeanne Gormick's search for God, enhanced by her Jewish faith, was inspiring. The book has wonderful examples of living life with a partner you love and are committed to, but don't share a mutual faith with."

Beryl Simmerok, Realtor

YOUR *Treasured* MARRIAGE

A God-Centered
Guidebook to Create
Long-Lasting Love

Jeanne Gormick

Your Treasured Marriage:
A God-Centered Guidebook to Create Long-Lasting Love

Aviva Publishing
Lake Placid, NY
518-523-1320
www.avivapubs.com

Copyright © 2022 Jeanne Gormick

All rights reserved, including the right to reproduce this book or any portion thereof in any form whatsoever. For information, address:

www.jeannegormick.com
jeanne@jeannegormick.com

All Scripture quotations, unless otherwise indicated, are taken from the Holy Bible, New International Version®, NIV®. Copyright ©1973, 1978, 1984, 2011 by Biblica, Inc.™ Used by permission of Zondervan. All rights reserved worldwide. www.zondervan.com The "NIV" and "New International Version" are trademarks registered in the United States Patent and Trademark Office by Biblica, Inc.™

Scripture taken from the Amplified Bible, Copyright © 2015 by The Lockman Foundation. Used by permission.

Scripture quotations marked (TLB) are taken from The Living Bible copyright © 1971. Used by permission of Tyndale House Publishers, Carol Stream, Illinois 60188. All rights reserved.

ISBN: 978-1-63618-191-2

Library of Congress: 2022908228
Editor: Sue A. Fairchild
Publishing Coach: Christine Gail
Cover Design and Interior Layout: Fusion Creative Works

10 9 8 7 6 5 4 3 2 1
First Edition, 2022

Printed in the United States of America

Dedication

To my late husband, Cal who shared this journey with me until the end and to Kirk who entered my love life two years later. I lost both of these great men way too soon.

A Note from My Daughter

In 2019, my mother, Jeanne Gormick, lost her best friend and husband of forty-nine years. My dad passed away from a heart attack just shy of their fiftieth wedding anniversary and seventieth birthdays. In the same year, my mother lost her special needs brother to abdominal cancer, her boobs to cancer, and her two nineteen-year-old cats.

After that much loss, a lot of people would shut down, become a recluse, or fall into the deepest of depression. And rightfully so.

But what did my mom do? She embraced this season in her life.

She joined a sailing club and a wine club, published two books, took her first ever solo road trip to South Dakota (Freaked me out, but she did great!), had her first drink of sake, started online dating (As much as we all terribly miss my dad, we are actually very supportive of our crazy/wonderful mom finding a partner to move forward with), started socially-distanced happy hours in her front yard with neighbors, started a virtual support group for grieving women, joined TikTok (Yes…TikTok. She's the "ClosetMillennial" because she feels like a Millennial trapped in the body of a 70-something-year-old woman), and much more.

Exactly three years after my dad passed away on January 14th, her new boyfriend of 8 months also sadly and unexpectedly passed away.

The bottom line is that Jeanne Gormick embraced life rather than letting it get her down when things have completely spiraled all around her.

Understandably grieving and mourning in her own way, she embraced each day and took every breathe as a blessing from God, wasting not one.

And this I find truly inspirational.

Julie Gormick Cox

Contents

Introduction	13
Chapter 1: First Date	15
Chapter 2: One Step Backward, Two Steps Forward	19
Chapter 3: The Lord's Timetable	27
Chapter 4: Day by Day … One Day at a Time	37
Chapter 5: What About the Children?	45
Chapter 6: Crossroads of Motherhood	51
Chapter 7: The Heart of My Personal Struggle	59
Chapter 8: Losing Self	73
Chapter 9: The Wise Woman Builds Her House	79
Chapter 10: Stop Being Superwoman and Start Being Faithful	93
Chapter 11: Submission	99
Chapter 12: Tough Choices to Make	105
Chapter 13: Crossroads of Marriage	113
Chapter 14: How the Scriptures Continued to Guide Me	121
Chapter 15: Hit From All Sides!	129
Chapter 16: This Old Age Thing is Getting Serious for Us, Too!	145
Chapter 17: The Roller Coaster Ride of Declining Health	149
Chapter 18: Going in Different Directions: Cal's Last Few Months	161
Chapter 19: The Lonesome Spiritual Journey	169

Chapter 20: Get to Know Your Husband's Family History	177
Chapter 21: Get to Know Your Husband's Position in His Family	183
Chapter 22: Get to Know Your Husband's Education and Career Background	187
Chapter 23: Get to Know Yourselves as a Couple – What are Your Personality Temperaments?	195
Chapter 24: Get to Know Yourselves as a Couple – Love Styles	201
Chapter 25: News Flash! Males and Females View Marriage Differently	205
Chapter 26: Get to Know Your Own Differences as Individuals	209
Chapter 27: Beware of Insecurities and Destructive Coping Mechanisms	215
Chapter 28: The Proverbs 31 Woman … Not Impossible with God	231
Conclusion: Love After Loss?	237
Acknowledgments	245
About the Author	247
Endnotes	249
Further Reading	257

Introduction

Stubborn, independent, impatient, and resistant to change—despite all these things, the Lord has chosen to use me! Through periods of extreme brokenness, the Lord has taken these negative qualities in me and turned them into good for his purposes.

After spending all twelve years of my married life as a Jew (by conversion), God called me to a personal relationship with him through his Son, Jesus.

The Lord brought me through several emotional crashes to new levels of faith. Up until then, I had only heard how spiritual growth through hurtful situations led others into spiritual maturity. I began to learn through my own painful experiences to die to my self and let God lead in order for me to become a useful vessel of his work for his purposes.

Stubbornness has become tenacity. Independence, over time, has been replaced by increased dependence upon God. And my resistance to change has opened up a new willingness to experience the exciting things the Lord has waiting for me. Only God Almighty could possibly do that!

But my journey has not been an easy one. I have tried, in my own strength, to live up to God's example of the perfect woman (Proverbs 31) and the world's Super Mom image, only to be continually discouraged. No doubt, women everywhere will identify with my struggles.

This journey and my growth with the Lord will not be over until I go home to be with him, and there will be continual ups and downs, but I have much to share and want to offer encouragement to women in all walks of life.

I was a home-based career woman for twenty-three years, who also worked in positions requiring the negotiation of rush hour traffic, so I can identify with both stay-at-home moms and working mothers. I've successfully survived the terrible twos, which, by the way, I found far more difficult than the teen years! The Lord has since brought our three Jewish children to a saving knowledge of their Messiah. Even with our major religious differences and the turbulent job losses of the 1990's, my husband, Cal, and I celebrated forty-nine years of marriage (and a little beyond) before I lost him. And our relationships with God grew. God can do anything!

Now, as I write this, a new chapter has begun in my life ….

Jeanne

Chapter 1

First Date

All around us, windows steamed while ours remained clear. From the standpoint of teens in the heat of passion, I suppose our car was one of the boring ones that cool November evening. We were having fun anyway!

The movie was *Judith*. The year was 1966.

Like most of the kids there, I can't remember details of the film we'd come to see, but not because we were steaming up the windows. Because we were hot and heavy into a deep discussion of religion. I had just discovered Cal Gormick, a guy I'd recently met at the Young Men's Christian Association (YMCA) teen program, was actually Jewish. I had always been drawn to Jewish boys—something my parents frowned upon.

After a pretty intense discussion about the Jewish faith, he turned to me as the movie was ending and asked if I would do him a favor.

"Of course," was my immediate response.

Then very seriously, very eloquently, he inquired, "Will you kiss me?"

How could I resist? This boy had such a special quality about him—a special gentleness—and, yet, so much life and energy. He certainly hadn't acted the way most guys act at a drive-in. He hadn't rushed at my body and pawed at me all night. He'd been my brother, my friend—such a refreshing change!

Oh, yes, I kissed him without a second thought and with as much passion as I was feeling at the moment. Later, he would describe that kiss as one from which he thought he'd never come up for air. Actually, it turned out to be far more passionate than I had expected. Not his passion, mine! I'd been taught not to kiss on the first date (after all, this was the mid-1960s).

I rationalized that I'd been a pretty good girl up to this point. And I really liked this guy. And it was only one kiss. But not one of those mechanical kisses you feel obligated to give on the second or third date just because it's expected. "This must mean something," I thought to myself.

The next day, I told my mother how special Cal was and how respectful he'd been. She was elated. But she was under the mistaken impression he was Catholic. His last name sounded Irish and he had red hair. I'm sure she felt relieved that, though she knew he wasn't an Episcopalian, she figured he was a Christian.[1]

I'd dated several really nice Jewish boys (one for two years) because I liked them better. In general, Jewish boys were more respectful and attentive to me. Probably because the Jewish culture puts family

---

1 Christian would have been the incorrect description anyway. Gentile would have been a more appropriate term since a Christian is not just someone who goes to church or was raised in a particular denomination. Actually, a better description might be "follower of Christ."

first. And I always had lots more fun with them. Years later, Cal proved my theory and became a faithful husband and wonderful father.

Cal's mother had a different reaction. She warned him he could be in for some real pain if my parents were against my dating Jewish boys. His parents suggested he nip the relationship in the bud. However, he, too, felt something special about us. He ignored his mother's warning and we began dating steadily. As his mom got to know me, she welcomed me with open arms.

That was the beginning of our fantastic life together.

Early in our relationship, I viewed Cal as my savior. I would have continued partying and drinking, and, perhaps, ventured into worse behaviors if Cal had not come into my life. He wasn't a party person, so he showed me how to have fun in new ways. He made it clear that he wasn't into partying and then showed me better ways to have fun like bowling, ice skating, supervised teen dances, etc. He accepted me for who I was.

As our relationship blossomed, I decided to convert to Judaism. My parents were not impressed.

Chapter Wrap-Up:

How did you meet your spouse or fiancé?

How might God be knocking at the door of your heart?

How have earthly relationships let you down?

Did you change anything about yourself to be part of the relationship? If so, what?

Describe a time you changed yourself for a relationship and then were let down by the relationship.

Chapter 2

One Step Backward, Two Steps Forward

Around age sixteen, my pilgrimage began.

I had been raised in the church by church-going parents. Both were active in the Episcopalian church. Dad served on the vestry (church board), was a lay reader, ushered, and taught Sunday school. Our mother volunteered in various capacities. My brothers and I were expected to follow in their footsteps. I remember longing to attend the adult discussion group instead of my boring Sunday school class. The adults discussed vital daily struggles and issues: the Vietnam War, church doctrine, religious theory—exciting issues that were important to my own search for truth.

My parents had difficulty comprehending my desire to engage in more in-depth conversation. "Until you're eighteen, you'll attend your own class," was repeated over and over. I had to settle for ridiculously earth-shattering dilemmas such as whether Johnny should go to the football game or to his tuba lesson!

The indirect stories were meant to lead students to make the right decisions. It just never related to me. It seemed to be too basic. I had a certain religious maturity even though I was only sixteen.

The closest Sunday school ever came to presenting a meaningful dialogue of consequence was when a visiting seminarian taught the class. His topic was "What Does It Mean to Be a Christian?" The assumption, of course, was that everyone in the room *was* a Christian. After all, everyone had been baptized and confirmed, including me. Then he made the statement that once you were baptized and confirmed into the Christian faith you would always be a Christian.

Scripturally, he was correct in that God does not take away salvation once given. The problem was that one must first be a committed believer in Christ through a personal confession of faith, not the confession of parents or peers.

I asked, "What would a Christian be if they became a Hindu, a Buddhist, or a Jew?"

My question threw him off because he had made an incorrect assumption about my commitment to the Lord.

After a thoughtful pause, he answered, "I guess you would be a bad Christian."

None of the other students seemed to share my disbelief in his answer. Like well-trained robots, they just sat there and accepted his teaching. I was *clearly* in the wrong place!

There was never any mention or explanation of a personal relationship with Jesus at that church. There was nothing to stimulate my thinking. We were only taught to obey, to follow in our parents' footsteps, and to accept what we were told. I knew then if I were ever to believe this stuff, I would have to find answers elsewhere. So, at age sixteen, I refused to attend my parents' church and began my own journey to find the one true God.

My first stop was the Unitarian church. A friend had invited me to attend with her family. My parents, finally respectful of my need to search, allowed me to go to this new church. They may have chosen to trust the Word of God which says,

> "Start children off on the way they should go, and even when they are old they will not turn from it." (Proverbs 22:6)

Nestled in the woods with a babbling stream nearby, I felt so close to God at the Unitarian church. The open glass windows allowed nature to come inside. I always made a point of sitting as close to the window as possible. I enjoyed watching squirrels, rabbits, and birds, the filtered sunlight on the leaves, the sparkling water, the rain, and the snow—everything! This place was so refreshing—nothing like the formal, rigid, cold, stone building I'd sat in Sunday after Sunday for so many years. (Years later I was reminded of this serene setting as three birds flew about inside the massive tent that housed Saddleback Church in Lake Forest, California.)

The Unitarian minister's views made much more sense too. He dealt with issues I'd longed to discuss in the adult discussion group. Moral values were taught without boring scriptural references. Scriptures never made any sense to me anyway. Who needed historical stories to keep man in his place! The Unitarian way was so much simpler and easier to comprehend.

(I learned later these external niceties did not lead to God either. Scriptural Truth provides the only answers. But on to the next port in this journey.)

I experienced a great deal of difficulty understanding and, therefore, accepting the Trinity. To me it violated the first commandment.

> "You shall not make for yourself an image in the form of anything in heaven above or on the earth beneath or in the waters below. You shall not bow down to them or worship them; for I, the Lord your God, am a jealous God, punishing the children for the sin of the parents to the third and fourth generation of those who hate me, but showing love to a thousand generations of those who love me and keep my commandments." (Exodus 20:4–6)

My search diverted toward a more familiar religion: teaching God's supremacy over man. That faith was Judaism. If, indeed, I were ever to find that Christianity was really the Truth, I would follow the route laid out by God. I joined a Hebrew caravan, hoping to trace the roots of Jesus, the "King of the Jews," the leader of the Christian faith. After all, Jesus was born of Jewish heritage and was culturally raised Jewish.

Shortly after beginning this religious pilgrimage, I began dating a Jewish boy named Chip. I seized the opportunity to attend temple services with his family. The services inspired me and drew me into the beauty of the Hebrew language. In the process, I determined the Unitarian church, in its attempt to intellectualize faith, did not fulfill my need for a more structured foundation.

However, Chip and his family weren't interested in helping me grow religiously. As a matter of fact, the whole two-year relationship with Chip was really shallow. We were just kids, and the love I felt for him was mere infatuation—an admiration for someone two years older. It was not the true, lasting love I would later discover. But nothing is ever wasted because this relationship introduced me to Judaism.

One month after Chip and I broke up (on the proverbial rebound), I met Cal. His mother's early reservations quickly turned to full acceptance. I think, in a way, our relationship helped her cope with the loss of her daughter, Bobbie, who had moved to California.

Cal's mother, Claire, was a wonderful, warm woman. I could see Cal got the same qualities from her. As I grew to know her, I identified more and more with her. As a writer, she expressed real emotion, something seemingly missing in my own home. I might as well have been her daughter. She was a mother the way I'd always wanted my mother to be—warm, loving, cuddly, physically affectionate, etc. Even the simple act of touching wasn't a comfortable, encouraged thing in my birth family. (As a result, I made a point of spending a lot of time touching each of my babies as they grew. I wanted them to experience my love through touch.)

My fiery temper and frustration with my own mother led to the day when I finally blurted out that Cal was also Jewish. In the heat of an argument with my mother, I practically spit the fact into her face. I was so frustrated that an evil-spirited response poured out. She really didn't deserve that kind of treatment.

Unfortunately, that outburst created a relationship of intense dislike between my mother and Cal—the antithesis of my relationship with his mother, Claire.

My mother always tried to live her life through me, but I needed to be me! She also failed to realize that I genuinely loved Cal. I know both my parents felt our relationship was some form of rebellion on my part. Who could blame them, the way I threw Cal up in their faces? They also showed great concern that he didn't believe Christ was God, but they didn't understand that I didn't either.

I'll be the first to agree that a relationship should be based on a certain number of important similarities along with the differences. For us, we really were identical in our faiths, a very important premarital concern. For followers of Christ, Scripture tells us

> "Do not be yoked together with unbelievers" (2 Corinthians 6:14a).

But we weren't unequally yoked! I was not even a Christian believer, let alone a follower of Christ!

Cal's family wasn't really strict in their faith. The kids had been educated in temple school and they'd received Bar and Bat Mitzvahs, but they weren't observant Jews. They were Reform Jews who taught their children to love God, but rarely attended services. As our relationship grew, I pressed Cal and his mother for information on conversion. Rabbi Maurice Davis agreed to teach me. This was relatively unusual since Judaism, unlike Christianity, does not seek converts. In fact, they discourage them.

This became my "One Step Backwards"—my search to return to Christ's beginnings as a Jew.

This made perfect sense to me because I had difficulty understanding the Trinity. I questioned, "Why the need for Jesus in addition to God Almighty?" Through conversion, I had found the only God I needed. I had no idea where this twist in the road would take me, but I made a full commitment to the Jewish faith and to Almighty God.

As I studied the Jewish faith, our relationship deepened, but was also tested. When I looked into colleges, I wanted to attend one 900 miles away, but I worried if our relationship would survive. I needed a breather from my parents' pressure against our relationship. Cal's mother commented, "If you are meant to be, your relationship will survive the separation." Those words permitted my final decision to choose that far-away college.

We parted just as we were realizing how deeply we cared for one another. Waiting for Christmas vacation was unbearable being so far away!

But after only one year of separation, Cal and I decided our commitment to each other had to be announced to the world and to my parents as soon as possible. Unlike other romantic proposals, Cal actually never asked me to marry him. Rather, he sent me a letter stating he wanted me to marry him and what did I think.

While Cal transferred home to continue his education, I began working to save for our upcoming marriage. We'd decided that announcing our marriage plans might convince my parents we were serious. I couldn't believe the pressure exerted by my parents during that time. They lied to Cal and told him my brother's epilepsy (caused by his DPT vaccination) was inheritable. I was told I could do so much better than Cal! And, though I didn't know it at the time, my parents actually offered Cal a blank check *not* to marry me.

Cal ethically declined the offer and, finally, one month before he returned to his junior year of college, we were married. Emotionally, we could no longer handle the external pressures placed on us by my parents, the threat of the Vietnam War draft, and school pressures.

Praise God, he helped our marriage to last even though we were both so young.

Chapter Wrap-Up:

Are you married to or dating an unbeliever? If so, how does that impact your own Christian walk?

What other relationships do you have with unbelievers? How does that impact your own faith?

Chapter 3

The Lord's Timetable

After spending the early days of our marriage attending the synagogue where we'd been married, Cal and I moved from New York to California. We experienced difficulty in locating a temple we liked, so we eventually stopped attending services together. We rationalized that our first child was still young, so it really didn't matter anyway. The only time we spent in services was at the Bar and Bat Mitzvahs for Cal's nieces and nephew.

However, as our children grew, I felt a greater need to provide them with a solid religious foundation. Since there was no Reform Temple near us, I returned to a nearby Unitarian church. Cal never felt comfortable there, so the kids and I attended alone for about a year. I taught Sunday school and the children grew, learning acceptable social values.

As a Sunday School teacher, however, I quickly discovered the problem with a church that tried to meet the religious needs of such a diverse population. The church had many people with different beliefs, including a Buddhist family. This meant even the Old Testament teachings were unacceptable. We didn't want to risk offending anyone.

Although the Unitarian concept of human acceptance seemed good on the surface, it just didn't provide concrete answers backed up with real proof. Morals and values were taught in the Unitarian church, but there was no specific basis for those teachings. Man loving his fellow man sounded good, but isn't in our human nature. In our natural state, we are only out for ourselves. Our children needed more structure than this environment could provide.

I was drawn to reinvestigate the Bible, but when I mentioned it at this church, I was discouraged. Scripture just had no place there. The Bible was considered a history book without any further meaning.

I was also deeply disturbed that our family, who did everything together, was not worshiping together. On Sundays, I would go off to church with our three kids and Cal would go out fishing. He often stayed out longer than our church service and, by the time we all returned home, the day was shot. Weekend family time had become even more important to us because I had recently returned to work full-time.

The church was drawing us apart instead of bringing us together.

Finally, the kids and I stopped attending the Unitarian church. Being together as a family was more religious and godlier than attending services as a partial family. I noticed many families splitting up around us, and it seemed a shame not to be a complete family in all our activities. So, the kids and I left the Unitarian church.

(I find it interesting that years later my focus became Trinitarian. Rather than focusing on the unity found in the one God, I discovered the concept of three in one within the tri-unity of our loving

God—God the Father, God the Holy Spirit, and God the Son. Yet He is still one God!)

Cal and I attended a coworker's birthday party where my religious search continued. I met a young man with whom I conversed about my favorite subject, religion. We went on for hours. Cal had learned long ago to leave me alone when I was expressing my intellectual opinions of religion. I shared with the young man that I would probably have become a Mormon, but that as a Jew I had an issue with their belief in Jesus. I was drawn to their philosophies of family togetherness, food storage, and some of their other disciplines. Of course, I was making generalized remarks about a faith of which I knew very little. I had no idea that their concept of Jesus is considerably different from that of mainline Christianity anyway.

The young man made a statement that I wrote off at the time, but now makes so much sense. He explained that one shouldn't choose one's religion or faith with their mind, but that it should come from one's heart.

I realize now that my mind had interfered with my true knowledge of the Lord for so many years. If I didn't understand something intellectually, it wasn't to be accepted. I had been influenced by external forces like the beautiful surroundings at my first Unitarian church. Even my adopted Judaism began with a feeling, a sense of awe. Slowly, praise God, his light was beginning to shine through, pricking deeply at my heart.

As the year continued, my path gradually became clearer. The previous year, I'd returned to full-time work in sales. The company was Christian-owned, but they never pushed their faith on me. Actually, they could have. I'd been so desperate to get out of the house and away from the kids, I was willing to put up with almost anything. My vain attempts to stimulate my own life with watercolor classes, stained glass classes, PTA meetings, and other volunteer activities just weren't enough! I wanted out! Though Cal warned me that their sales meetings might involve prayer, I found only respect there. No one ever imposed his or her beliefs on the employees.

(Looking back, there is no question in my mind that this company was exactly where God wanted me at that precise moment of my life. God's timing is always so miraculous.)

I was excited to be beginning the career I'd waited so long for. Finally, our family timing seemed right for me to return to full-time employment. I'd desperately looked to be out of the "just a house-wife" syndrome.

When our daughter was just two, I'd had a fantastic opportunity to pursue a position as a Market Research Project Director. The job seemed perfect for me. I would use my years of market research management in the home-based environment to move up the career ladder to be someone—not just a housewife with a part-time job. I couldn't wait to get on with my life!

However, as happens so often, I could not justify leaving our two-year-old daughter in childcare. She was a demanding, attached two-year-old and clearly needed me. That's why I needed out, but it was also why I couldn't leave her.

I felt so depressed by not being able to move forward in my career that I shut down for two solid weeks and did nothing. Cal did the laundry, the cooking ... everything! I was so sad, so alone. But God was working his timetable for my life, even back before I knew him. So, I waited.

Three years later, Todd was firmly established in school, Julie was a happy, independent child heading off to kindergarten, and Tim was an outgoing, energetic two-year-old ready for preschool. I was finally ready to escape and get on with my life! Sounds pretty harsh, but as a young mother who didn't have the love of Jesus in her life yet, unfortunately, it's where I was at the time.

As I began my new career in title insurance sales, I absorbed myself in motivational tapes and books to help me increase my sales performance. These motivational materials led me to a renewed religious awareness. This time, however, my life was going better than ever. I'd just had my most productive month at work. My husband and kids were healthy and happy. We were about to purchase our dream house. I was feeling fulfilled for the first time in my life and the last thing on my mind was God. Little did I know that I was to be drawn from that moment on into his wonderful presence.

So many seemingly unrelated things began to happen, one right after the other.

A new Reform Jewish Temple was being organized close to our home. Since the kids were getting older, we wanted them to have a solid religious foundation, so we joined the temple.

The Christmas before, a card from a close high school buddy revealed that she'd recently become "born again." I felt sorry for her, but at the same time felt angry. How could she have fallen for all that religious stuff? She just wasn't the type! With my brother and parents anything was possible, but with Angie it was inconceivable!

She mentioned the Living Bible, that it was easy to read and made everything so clear to her but, of course, I didn't need any of that. I was a Jew and had chosen to be one after four years of careful investigation. I don't take these important decisions lightly.

About this time, my "born again" Christian brother had sent me an interesting book by Hal Lindsey entitled, *The Late Great Planet Earth*. I was fascinated by the ideas presented in the book concerning the theoretical end of the world known as "Armageddon." I couldn't believe the biblical references were from the same Bible I'd had growing up. Remembering what Angie had shared about the Living Bible, I bought one as a reference tool. That purchase was to be my first true turning toward God.

My sales manager, Tom, suggested I read Rev. Robert Schuller's book *Possibility Thinking*. That led me to tune into his *Hour of Power* TV program.

Two books entered my life around this time: *The Dynamic Laws of Prosperity* and *The Powers of the Subconscious Mind*. The spiritual "truths" within each were lightly religious but, surprisingly, I didn't find them offensive. The Bible quotations used seemed to be so sensible.

I was amazed that most references were from the New Testament, things Jesus had taught. They demonstrated how the Christian orientation would help me in sales. Though I later discovered that such teaching is potentially dangerous, I was being instructed to pray in a way I'd never done before—every step of the way. I learned to pray that I would say just the right thing during a sales call. I learned to use (what I thought was) the Lord's power to handle life's everyday situations.

I felt fantastic! God was always with me this way not just when I needed him, but always. He soon became my personal friend and it felt good to have a friend in such a high place. Someone to help me achieve success. I prayed for him to come to me for help time and time again.

Sometimes this whole period of my life doesn't make much sense. The lord I was asking help from may not have been the one True God. If nothing else, I was wrong to use the Lord for selfish gain. Somehow the real God took all of this and placed it in the right order to bring me to him. These diverse spiritual materials refueled my religious search. I checked out quotations for myself and found others of interest. As I read the easily understood text, God slowly began to reveal his true power in a mighty way.

> "Ask and you will be given what you ask for. Seek, and you will find. Knock, and the door will be opened. For everyone who asks, receives. Anyone who seeks, finds. If only you will knock, the door will be opened." (Matthew 7:7–8 TLB)

Over the following summer, I felt God calling me.

I was okay with being called as long as Jesus Christ wasn't a part of it! Though I was born gentile, and in the minds of many, was a Christian, I was committed to my adopted Jewish faith.

Then, I remembered something about Cal's mother who had died seven years before. She had tried to explain to me that there were Jews who believed Jesus was the Messiah. Uncomfortable with the topic, I quickly changed the subject. We never discussed it further, but, apparently, she had begun to visit a group of Jewish believers. Though she never discussed her beliefs with us, I now know in my heart she knew her Messiah.

About a year and a half after her death, my father-in-law, Barney, met and married a lovely Hebrew-Christian woman who had been brought to the Lord by her children. Then, that same year, my deeply troubled brother suddenly wrote that Jesus had made a great change in his life. The following year my parents wrote that they, too, had been "born again." The handwriting was on the wall, but it all made me feel *so* uncomfortable. I felt glad they were all 3,000 miles away.

Then came the "Invasion of the Christians." Wherever I went, Christians came out of the woodwork—the salesgirl, friends we'd known for years, a girl I worked with, a client. I couldn't believe it! I think I knew what God wanted, but I was *so* unsure. And yet, it all seemed so simple! For years I'd intellectualized and investigated, but accepting the gift God had for me by sincerely confessing my sins and asking Jesus into my heart to guide me along his path for my life was simple.

I had read I should share my new faith, my new thoughts, and my new Jesus, so I ventured out and told one of our friends, Teri, what was going on. As I explained my emerging Christian belief, she shared hers with me.

God's communiqué was undeniable by now, but I was terrified by the obvious direction God wanted for my life. What would happen to my relationship with Cal? How would he react to having his wife turn into a "born again Christian," the very thing that, together, we had criticized others for.

Finally, I became so frustrated with myself that I simply reached out in faith to trust the Lord. I made my commitment to him and made a deal that I would believe, if he would help me tell Cal. That night a small voice within me, like the one that spoke to Elijah, when the Lord appeared to him on the mountain (1 Kings 19:12), kept nagging at me until I finally gave in. My response came in the form of a challenge to just jump in and believe.

I responded to God, "Okay, God, if this Jesus stuff is real, go ahead, come into me!"

I was familiar with the salvation prayer (confessing my lifelong wrongdoings and asking Jesus to take over my life) from some information my mother had sent me years before.

I continued, "I suppose I've sinned, though I didn't know it, and if I have, I'm sorry and I hope that's enough."

On that statement, I went to sleep thinking something very wonderful was happening to me.

Through God's grace, he revealed himself to me. But I had to learn to stop walking in old ways. (Romans 6:1-2)

Chapter Wrap-Up:

How have you felt God pulling at you to change or grow your relationship with him?

How have you avoided God in the past? If so, what were the consequences?

How does God communicate with you?

Chapter 4

Day by Day ... One Day at a Time

The next morning after my sin confession, serious fears enveloped me.

"I can't do this! Cal and I are so close. Our marriage is great; why mess it up? This will destroy everything and put so much pressure on our relationship. I can't do this!"

I had to be sure this was real. I had to be sure the Christian direction was the right one for me. It had to be right. However, there had been just too many coincidences and then all those Christians around me. I couldn't, I wouldn't, call myself a believer until I was really sure. Even though I'd pretty much accepted all God had laid out for me, I talked with Christian friends about "working toward being a Christian," but not about already being one. I spoke to Chris, one of the first Christian friends I'd made. I shared with her my fear to trust the Lord in all of this. Intellectually, I was frustrated because I knew if I believed, then the Lord would provide. But I was still afraid to believe, afraid to trust fully.

Then my first identifiable communication with the Lord happened.

On the morning of September 3, 1981, as I drove to see my first client, I confessed the sins in my life and prayed for Jesus to *really* enter my heart. I promised I would follow him, but that I was still afraid of Cal's reaction. I prayed for an answer. I was still shaky in my trust of his power over mine, but I had to start somewhere.

By four that afternoon, I'd forgotten my morning prayer as I walked up to the last real estate client for the day, Jim Alessi. I had never met him before, but I noticed he was reading a psychology book about the theories of Jung. As a psychology major, I immediately recognized the work of a noted psychologist, so I asked Jim about it. The dialogue that followed was nothing short of miraculous to me.

I inquired, "Are you studying for a class or something? That's pretty heavy stuff."

He replied that he was comparing what a famous psychologist had said to what Jesus said in the Bible. I asked several questions, thoroughly fascinated with his views.

Somewhere in our conversation, the Lord began to provide the answer to my prayer of that morning.

I was in disbelief! Here was yet another "surprise" Christian—one I'd never even met before. I thought Jim might even be an angel!

Ignoring cautions that business and religion don't mix, I opened my heart to Jim and explained my fears.

After listening to me intently, he said, "You must do what is best for you and trust God to handle the rest."

The words were simple, but oh, how true!

I was elated as I left Jim's office and drove toward home. Jim was the first of many catalysts the Lord used to bring me closer to him.

I was terribly excited and really wanted to share all I had learned with Cal. However, I also understood how this conversion would appear to him. I prayed for guidance on how to tell him. I couldn't just be open and share. I knew this was a "born again" experience, but we'd both been so turned off by people who said they were born again. Now I was one of those people! I was so afraid I would have to choose between Cal and Jesus. I couldn't handle that. We'd been married for twelve years and close friends around us were divorcing at the drop of a hat. I didn't want to risk the good relationship we had. Too new in the faith, I couldn't see that God also desired to protect our precious bond. As my girlfriend, Angie, later explained, God is *not* in the divorce business. Slowly, the Lord helped me gain confidence in his great power.

God provided the perfect opportunity to share my new faith with Cal in a way that only God could have designed. I got the idea to buy a simple gold cross as a symbol of my new faith. Gradually, I gained the confidence to wear the necklace so Cal might see it. I'd finally decided to just walk in faith. After all, if God had created this entire world, he was certainly able to protect and guide me in this simple situation.

Unfortunately, when I opened the door to the house, I chickened out! I put the cross under my blouse. Later, I covered myself with my bathrobe, pulling the left and right sides to my chin with more modesty than a virginal, new bride! I waited for Cal to get into bed first and then made sure the light was out. When I got into bed, I realized how ridiculous this was becoming, I gave the situation back to the Lord, vowing not to retreat again.

I wore the cross openly from that moment on.

By the next day, Cal hadn't noticed anything when we got a call that his father was hospitalized and about to undergo open-heart surgery. Three days later, Cal still hadn't noticed the cross.

"Maybe we're playing some kind of game," I thought. "He must have seen it. I'm not hiding it."

The following day, five-year-old Julie noticed the cross and asked, "Is that Jewish?"

I told her we would talk about it later after I spoke with Daddy about it. I explained that God was sharing something very special with me.

As Cal's dad entered surgery, I had a moment to speak with his wife, Dottie (a Jewish believer). I told her I had a Bible if she needed it. We talked briefly about what had happened to me. Amazingly, she indicated her daughter, Suzie, thought I might be able to help Dottie deal with the religious differences in the family. This was before I'd even told Dottie that I had become a new believer! God must have communicated with Suzie about my emerging faith. I didn't understand it all, but I knew God would get me through it.

The next few days were difficult. I'd begun to dwell on negative things—Dad's condition, our finances, etc. I began to feel hopeless. I figured this must be some kind of test of my faith. This doubt only lasted a day and a half before the Lord's warm glow and inner confidence returned. I felt much better.

Those Christian believers still kept popping up just when I needed them. Nancy, from Chris's office, struck up a conversation about my new faith. I told her about the hopeless feelings I'd had. She explained that my humanism was just rising up. It was natural. She assured me that God knew my heart. I learned that though Jesus enters our hearts, we remain human and have to deal with our own evil within. We prayed together that the Lord would bring Cal along with me on my Christian journey.

The next week, Cal and I visited his dad in the hospital. Cal and I just couldn't communicate. It was awful! I knew he was upset about his dad, but I kept arguing with everything he said.

The next day I apologized to him and spoke briefly about God.

He said, "I hope you're not becoming involved in some religious thing."

I told him I'd just been investigating spiritual things and had discovered I hadn't been listening to my heart. I felt God was a whole lot closer and less abstract than I had thought. I explained that he was much more than just the Creator. He is someone I could call on daily, moment by moment. I expressed that I had found the full power and love of God.

The conversation switched to the dream house we'd almost purchased. I explained that the books I'd been reading had basically said I could have anything I wanted, if I only believed myself having it. I told Cal I'd been wrong. I didn't have that kind of power! I explained that only God has that kind of power. I apologized to Cal for any responsibility I'd had in pushing for that house. What a blessing that we didn't buy it! We would have needed my income to purchase it and, unknown to me, I was not to have my job for much longer. We didn't see any of that, but, praise God, he did!

The truth finally came out the following day.

Cal's dad called from the hospital. During the conversation his dad mentioned that Cal's sister, Bobbie, had seen a cross around my neck. Cal assured his dad I didn't have on a cross. When he got off the phone, I knew we had to talk. God had opened the door.

In between tears of fear, sadness, and joy, I explained I'd wanted to talk with him for the last few weeks. I told him what had been happening to me ever since the day before Dad had entered the hospital. I explained about the spiritual growth I'd had over the past five months. I stressed that no one had pressured me, but that many had encouraged me.

Cal became very defensive about Jesus. He wanted to know what I now believed. I answered that I believed *Yeshua*, Jesus, the Living God, was the Messiah and that he lived and died and is alive for me now.

I assured Cal to not worry about our relationship. My desire was to get the family more involved in the Temple. I would encourage them to be as Jewish as possible to fulfill Bible prophecies. I was a bit off base, being new to the faith, but I told him what I understood this to mean back then. His reply was that he wasn't concerned about our relationship, but he asked me very firmly never to talk about Jesus with him.

I'd experienced no sudden appearance of the Lord Jesus standing in front of me. God's loud voice didn't come booming down at me. He came as a gentle knocking on the door of my heart. My desire is to share that quiet knocking, so others will also hear and recognize it for their own lives.

Following my encounter with God, the Father of Abraham, Isaac and Jacob, and his precious Son, Jesus, our life did change. In God's slow and loving way, Cal did come to understand what I had to do and I learned how to handle the new faith.

In each situation, one by one God solved difficulties in the best way.

Chapter Wrap-Up

What have you ever been afraid to trust God for?

How has God answered prayer for you?

Chapter 5

What About the Children?

At first I decided to leave the children's religious upbringing as it was. They would be raised Jewish (as Jesus was) and I wouldn't rock the boat. This was a purely human decision on my part.

As time went on and I matured in my new faith, I desired them to become believers and followers of Christ and to be raised as such. However, each time I ventured in these directions, the Lord stopped it.

I always asked Cal if I could take the kids to church activities and he often agreed. However, one time we arrived early to pick them up. Cal was offended by the concluding songs and prayers which included mentions of "Jesus". Unfortunately, the kids weren't permitted to return.

Finally, I began to receive loving "expressions" from God, telling me they were to be raised Jewish and that he (not I) would take them where he wanted them. I would one day have three Hebrew-Christian children, just like Jesus. This was confirmed in several ways. First, the Lord gave me an interesting Scripture. It really described my own life.

> "Yet to all who received him, to those who believed in his name, he gave the right to become children of God—children born *not of natural descent, nor of human decision* or *a husband's will,* but *born of God.*" (John 1:12–13 emphasis mine)

I had done everything in my own life, in my own strength to be one of God's chosen people. But only God has the power to make us his children! Though our kids had received that privilege directly from God (by birth), they were not yet his children. My instructions seemed clear. Shortly after receiving the Lord into my heart, I began sensing God's direction through his Holy Spirit. The Lord touched my heart and told me he would take my children where he wanted them.

More than a year later he provided a Scripture to back up his commandment to me…

> "Each person should remain in the situation they were in when God called them." (1 Corinthians 7:20)

My situation was that I was married to a Jewish man. We had three Jewish children (by birth, since I was Jewish when they were born and they were being raised as Jews at the time of my own conversion experience). My instructions were clearly to remain where God had already placed me. I had no other choice, nor did I desire to do anything other than to raise them Jewish.

Almost two years after I had found Messiah Jesus, Timmy (our youngest) started asking all kinds of deep questions. We were in the car and I answered without paying much attention to what he was really asking. Before I knew it, he asked me how he could be a Christian. As the teacher of two-year-old children at my church, I explained the salvation prayer in language he could understand. I explained he had to apologize to God for all the bad things he'd done and then ask Jesus to come into his heart. He requested that we pray that prayer. As I parked the car, I worried how Cal would respond to this, but I trusted God. Timmy and I asked Jesus into his heart.

Over the next few months, he began praying for his daddy to know Jesus, to have Jesus come into his daddy's heart. I was amazed as Timmy explained that he didn't want his daddy to die. He wanted him to live forever with Jesus. From somewhere, Timmy had gotten all his facts straight, just as if he'd been in Sunday school all his life. A few days later I found a Scripture describing what had just happened to Timmy.

> "No longer will they teach their neighbor, or say to one another, 'Know the Lord,' because they will all know me, from the least (youngest) of them to the greatest (oldest)." (Hebrews 8:11 additions mine)

I was so excited and kept praising God for his faithfulness!

Daughter Julie says now, "I thought it worked well between you and Dad because you always did everything out of respect for him. If we, as kids, wanted to go to church with you in the early days you would always have us ask Dad. He would always say yes (with a bit of a guilt trip), but it was a level of respect from my perspective."

Sending the kids to ask their dad for church things was the best guidance the Holy Spirit gave me. And over these many years, God has always been faithful in his protection and provision through his tremendous love for us. I knew in my heart that someday he would fulfill his special promises for my family all to know him.

Julie posted this on her Facebook one Easter.

> "Jesus said to her, 'I am the resurrection and the life. The one who believes in me will live, even though they die; and whoever lives by believing in me will never die. Do you believe this?'" (John 11:25–26)

Being raised Jewish, this was one holiday that growing up always made me a little sad. For some reason, we celebrated Christmas (with Hanukkah … the Christmas tree was the "Hanukkah Bush" Lol.), but never Easter. Easter was for the 'other people,' not us. As a child I didn't understand this. I just knew that all of my friends got Easter baskets and candy and got to have Easter egg hunts, and we did not.

Even after giving my heart to Jesus at twelve years old, it took me years to feel like this day was for me too. At twelve years old, after hearing the story of salvation and given an opportunity to invite Jesus into my heart as my personal Lord and Savior, I didn't walk up to the stage at church camp with other the kids. But I did say the name of Jesus in my head for the first time without denying it. (Prior I would denounce his Name every time someone spoke it, feeling bad and feeling like I was going against my Jewish faith and letting God and my family down because Jesus was for the 'other people,' not us. So, I said his Name in the silence of my heart. And he has continued to reveal himself to me daily ever since.

Today, my heart is full. Jesus has completed me. The Messiah, the Son of the Living God."

This is such an encouragement that I want to share with parents concerned about their children growing in and staying with the Lord. God is good! He will never let you down. He knows your heart!

Years ago, I wrote in my journal my belief (and prayer) that Cal and Todd would both be brought into a saving knowledge and personal relationship with Jesus Christ too.

Todd, who had been Bar Mitzvahed at age thirteen, became a Catholic as he started his marriage with Heather.

Chapter Wrap-Up

How are you instructing your children to know the Lord's laws?

Do you have a life verse or special Scripture(s) that describes your life with Christ? Write out in the space provided.

_____
_____
_____
_____
_____

If you have concerns for your children, read Proverbs 22:6 for encouragement.

Chapter 6

Crossroads of Motherhood

After the Lord entered my life as my personal Lord and Savior, my eyes were really opened. One afternoon I was eating lunch by myself when I noticed the trees blowing gently outside the window. I thought of how God's creation is so amazing. On the trees outside, each leaf flowed in its own way, each one, so different—an olive tree, a pine tree, an acacia. Even the sun shone differently on each. I noticed the sounds around me—the voices, the silverware being set out, the hum of the kitchen machinery, dishes clanging, gentle music playing. I suddenly understood how much I had to block out just to get through each working day. I was always in a rush, running here and there, with no time to "stop and smell the roses."

I needed to reassess my life. I wasn't like everyone else! Like the leaves, we are each so different. Our needs and responsibilities differ. Our kids (aged three, six, and nine at the time) needed a mother who cared, who had the time to be there for them (in more than mere presence). My workaholic nature persuaded me to work past the hours of others in my profession. As the kids grew older, their needs increased. They had more homework and the problems they faced each day were becoming more and more complex. No longer would a simple soothing kiss be sufficient.

Three months after I became a believer, the economy threatened my beloved career. God placed me at a crossroads. I had to make the decision to quit or hold on to my job, hoping things would improve. They removed my company car and put me on straight commission. I would no longer have the guaranteed income needed to pay for Timmy's preschool. God clearly showed me I had to leave for a very practical reason. It was extremely difficult for me, but I knew I was being taught an important lesson about love, relationships, and obedience. I knew I had to quit.

As we drove away from returning my company car, Cal said, "It will be nice to get back to being a simple family again. This will bring us back together." Later that night, he said, "You've taken a big step forward today."

He knew how difficult it had been for me to quit the job I loved so much, but this was my first indication that Cal wasn't happy about my career choices. For the first time, I saw where we might have been headed. When I think of what I could have lost, I can only praise God for rescuing me before it was too late.

Shortly after I quit that precious job, Cal was blessed with a new position paying as much as our combined income had been and we started a family business on the side. It became pretty obvious we were being blessed through my obedience!

In *The Family: God's Masterpiece* by Helen Duff Baugh, the mother's role is described as being "the 'heart' of the home, (she creates) the atmosphere of the home."[1]

During these times of growth and struggle I developed a new patience level. It allowed me to see the entire picture before losing my temper with the kids. I recall one night we came home to find the sitter mopping up a shattered bottle that had broken my best sugar bowl. Before, I would have simply blown up. This time, thankfully, I got the details first. Todd, our oldest, was just trying to get a cookie for his little brother, Timmy, to take to bed, when his arm hit the bottle that broke the sugar bowl.

I also learned patience in answering the persistent questions children ask.

I still remember attempting to answer seven-year-old Julie's questions when I told her that God was everywhere.

"Is he in the refrigerator?"

To which I responded, "I guess so. He is everywhere."

"Does he get cold in there?" Before I could respond, she continued, "If he's in the refrigerator, is he behind the milk or the pickles?"

In desperation, my answer was, "I don't know!"

Finally, she opened the refrigerator door to search for God herself. Had this occurred just a few short months before, I might have missed the opportunity all together or scurried her off to play without continuing the discussion. This time I was able to relish the joy provided by the episode. (Julie's search for God ended at age twelve when she found a personal relationship with her Messiah, Jesus.)

Those many years ago my world became filled with important little things—stopping to watch a ladybug crawl across a flower or seizing a chance to truly absorb and answer little Timmy's many and varied questions. I was so glad to be an important part of his life again. Being a closer part of the kids' lives gave me opportunities to instill values in them, to answer their important questions my way and God's way. I got to know my kids again!

The kids and I did things I just didn't have time for before. I treasure those fleeting moments now that the kids are grown with children of their own. I learned important things like how to make play dough from scratch and something called "flub." I learned you can make butter by shaking and shaking and shaking heavy cream in a jar until it separates into butter and nonfat milk. Lessons for our kids became lessons for me.

At a Florence Littauer CLASS Seminar, Florence shared the importance of writing down all the little things that go on in our daily lives. I'm so glad I wrote down some of them. Journaling the things that happened in my everyday life has permitted me to relive those precious moments. I also included biblical insights I learned as I did my daily Bible studies, as well as prayer requests and the results.

What a wonderful legacy to share with our children and grandchildren! I still journal daily.

I felt compelled to write this part of my story because if I can help another young mother understand the importance of really being there for her kids, my painful experiences will have been worth it all.

I discovered many options to be a working, stay-at-home mom with a home-based business. I determined that my outside career goals needed to be postponed for as long as possible. The rewards our little ones provided were numerous, but so temporary. I learned to "hang in there!" Material sacrifices are definitely worth the struggle. I surrounded myself with others desperately fighting the "just a housewife syndrome." This helped with the loneliness and isolation I sometimes felt. While the world tells us we need more and more things, these things are often acquired at the expense of our most important relationships.

If you are in a position to change your attitudes and circumstances, please consider it. If, as a single mom, you have no other options, the Lord will care for your children when they are in someone else's care. He knows your heart!

NOTE: Prayer can change circumstances and protect your family.

I can't claim my transition back to the home was easy. I didn't always find the loving family support I needed, but the Lord got me through the most trying of times. With the Lord's help and guidance, I survived and have thrived through it all.

Looking back, I never would have dreamed that there could be fulfillment in a trip to the zoo, doing tens loads of laundry a week, and cooking, baking, cleaning, ironing, or chauffeuring children to their various activities. I actually found joy in these activities and in trying to see how much money I could save by using coupons. My flexible hours and home-based business location permitted me the time I needed to shop for sales. I couldn't do that while working on someone else's timetable.

I quickly discovered I could turn my hobbies of stained glass, writing, and, later, antique collecting into moneymaking ventures. My efforts in the housework department never achieved perfection, but my family had changed.

The heart of our house was, again, filled with love. Cal began to make comments like, "You seem calmer and less hassled when I come home now." What a nice way for a husband to come home! We noticed that Timmy's behavior also improved. He and I were able to attend a parent participation preschool together. While I worked outside the home, Timmy rarely had my individual, undivided attention. No wonder he had learned to do such negative things just to get my attention. He really only needed a mom who wasn't so busy satisfying her own needs that she failed to understand his.

I am only sharing what God had to do in my life to bring me to a place of brokenness in obedience and yielding to him. Each person's situation is different. I had to be completely broken before I could release complete control of my life to him. God's direction became much clearer, but to this day I still struggle to deny myself (Luke 9:23.)

Even later owning my own PR company became an issue in my life. Following the closure of my own company, I returned to the workforce as an employee and became a church secretary. By then the kids were almost all out of the house. All my entrepreneurial desires and energies became focused on God's will for my life. I was removed from the temptation of making my business an idol, as I had with owning my own business, when I had become an employee at a church, no less! In *Faith That Follows,* author Seth Ebel says, "Sometimes we look to other things to satisfy and fulfill us—to 'save' us. These 'functional saviors' can be any object of dependence we embrace that isn't God. They become the source of our identity, security, and significance because we hold an idolatrous affection for them in our hearts. They preoccupy our minds and consume our time and resources. They make us feel good and somehow even make us feel righteous. Whether we realize it or not, they control us, and we worship them."[2]

But as I share in other chapters, jobs and my own business quickly became idols as I began advancing in my career.

This is a lifelong, difficult and, at times, trying process. I had to experience this struggle in order to grow as a faithful follower of Christ. I believe it was God's method of showing me over and over again that my own business and career goals had become idols. Amazingly, there is always a new lesson he has for me no matter where he puts me!

Chapter Wrap-Up:

Have you ever tried journaling? It can be helpful as you look back and see how the Lord has gotten you through life's difficulties.

Have you considered starting your kids on journaling?

How does your career affect your childrearing?

How might your career (or even your family) actually be an idol in your life that takes you away from God or family responsibilities?

Chapter 7

The Heart of My Personal Struggle

I was reflecting on yet another of my unsuccessful job situations where the Lord had humbled me and protected our marriage relationship.

As the kids got older, I ventured back into the workplace with a market research management position at the local mall. I loved working with the young staff and using my Christian values to follow the strict requirements of market research. During one particular survey, we were having difficulty finding respondents. When I spoke to my boss's assistant in the home office back east, I was told to just make up fictitious surveys to meet the quota by deadline.

I refused to do that, but had no way to contact my boss who was traveling. All communication went through her assistant.

I loved the job, but because of the assistant's insistence for me to falsify the data, my ethics, standards, and orientation to detail were under attack. As a Christian believer, I was going through a tremendous trial and time of testing. Only God could create something good from something bad, as his Word says. But God *did* have greater plans—plans I couldn't see!

> "For it is God who works in you to will and to act in order to fulfill his good purpose." (Philippians: 2:13)

We can't do it on our own. We need his power for his plan to be complete. Even to begin our journey toward his will and his plan for our lives, we always need to draw on his power.

Later, I discovered seeds I'd sown in the life of one of my twenty-year-old staffers had come to harvest. I heard that he had become a believer. That news made much of my own personal pain and stress worth the struggle. All the pain I'd experienced finally seemed to have been turned to good by the Lord.

At the worst of that trial, when I had truly reached bottom, I didn't care if I ever worked again. Being stripped of my professional dignity *did* help to mold me into being a stronger follower of Christ—one much more dependent upon God. It reminded me of how the Israelites fought God's ways.

> "Yet they rebelled and grieved his Holy Spirit. So he turned and became their enemy and he himself fought against them." (Isaiah 63:10)

> "Yet, as they recalled what the Lord had done for them over the years, they returned to him and were given rest by the Spirit of the Lord." (Isaiah 63:14).

This is how the Lord guided his people to make for himself a Glorious Name. I, too, had received his rest for the moment.

As hard as it was for me to wait and not do anything in my own strength, my husband, Cal, was taking over. Wow—I was also learning to submit to him, the man the Lord had given to me so many years before.

Just ten days after receiving what I thought was a clear message from the Lord to stay in that position, he released me from the job through Cal, who was extremely concerned for my well-being and insisted that I file a disability claim.

Though I never wanted something I wasn't entitled to, Cal convinced me to go onto stress-related disability for a short time until I could heal.

My career continued when I became a Regional Director with another company. I enjoyed that position, though there was tremendous pressure to bring in weekly sales.

Then, at age fifty-six, Cal had his first heart attack. Our kids were grown at the time, but seeing him in the hospital hooked up to tubes and a breathing machine alerted me to possibly facing life without him—an eye-opening moment. All the struggles we'd had in our differences were suddenly focused in the reality of loss. I developed a very new appreciation for him during this time.

A month after this health scare, I left this sales job to care for Cal and re-group. At the time, I had no idea if I would qualify for unemployment insurance or not. I just knew Cal needed me and I had to get out of a stressful situation.

I was eventually blessed with favor from the State Unemployment judge who determined that, indeed, I did qualify for unemployment because the job had changed for my situation. And as Cal recovered, I accepted a job at a magazine but a month later my new boss told me, "This just isn't working out."

With Cal's health issues and mounting bills, I hadn't spent time praying for the right job. I just took the first job that I was offered.

Not involving the Lord caused yet another blow to my pride! This really hit me hard because I've never had a job that didn't work out due to any imperfection on my part. This occurred in October. As the holidays approached without other job prospects in sight, Cal reassured me we had money in the bank and not to worry about getting another job until after the holidays.

I felt abandoned, rejected, tossed away, lost. I'd never been fired before! This finally made me *ready* to rest in the arms of God.

I had to trust that the Lord would bring me just the right job, in his time and in his way. Going through my journal notes for this book, I noticed all the problems I'd experienced in the workplace and was reminded that each effort I'd made toward working in the marketplace had been in vain. I had always been relying on my own decisions without involving God's wisdom and direction.

> "Unless the LORD builds the house, the builders labor in vain. Unless the LORD watches over the city, the guards stand watch in vain. In vain you rise early and stay up late, toiling for food to eat—for he grants sleep to those he loves." (Psalm 127:1–2)

The Lord stopped me in my tracks during this healing process and led me to another amazing discovery.

Though I'd believed in Christ for many years, I realized that through my desire to control sometimes (maybe most times?) I had become my own Lord and Savior! I had been striving to maintain the control of my life. Those days of job stress were due to my continual attempt to hold onto what was God's—my failure to fully release every area of my life to him. By doing this, I was actually denying him, as had the church in Crete (Titus 1:16).

Because our Lord loves us so much, he often disciplines us through seemingly unbearable, uncomfortable trials to bring us closer to him. Another of my pastors, explained it this way, "We don't break God's law, his law breaks us." Out of God's will, no choice is the right one, but within God's will every choice is protected. His love for me, coupled with my own desire to know him better, resulted in genuine progress as I grew in "wisdom and stature in favor with God and man" like Jesus (Luke 2:52).

During this new time of seeking the Lord, I determined to sit each morning and read the Bible, but I found my brain wanted to get on with my day! Over many months of persistent practice, I began to crave my time in the Word and the struggle lessened. Now, when I don't get that time, for whatever reason, I miss that quiet time.

I finally began seeing my life through God's eyes, not my own! But I still have so far to go.

Our walks with Jesus are truly journeys and as I prayed and studied his Word I began to see the reason my previous jobs all seemed to collapse. I was seeking them out in my own strength, not God's. Even though I was doing good things, I had been doing them without the guidance of the Holy Spirit—without his perfect timing.

> "I am the true vine, and my Father is the gardener. He cuts off every branch in me that bears no fruit, while every branch that does bear fruit he prunes so that it will be even more fruitful." (John 15:1–2)

> "Whoever heeds discipline shows the way to life, but whoever ignores correction leads others astray." (Proverbs 10:17)

This combined process of growing in the Lord and my experiencing workplace disasters forced me to soul search, to continually re-evaluate my journey with Christ. God wanted me to find my own answers directly from God's own words in the Bible and from his Holy Spirit.

A pastor from Celebration Christian Center once summed it up like this: "Life will break you, but we must learn to break into the hands of God. He's just waiting for that brokenness. Then he can begin to do something in our lives."

I could not do this in my own strength.

It seemed clear that the Lord wanted something different from me. During this latest job loss, I re-organized and re-painted the house and Cal and I did some volunteer work. I was trying to use my time well as I sought the Lord's will. Over the years, when in faithful obedience I waited for the Lord's timing and direction, things always seemed to go better. Finally, I acknowledged I must always involve the Lord in every single life decision.

I was excited and feeling rewarded by my godly obedience when I became Vice President of Community Relations for a homecare company.

Once I was situated, Cal admitted that being on Social Security Disability Insurance (SSDI) might be the only way for him to go. Because of his ill health, he had to take daily naps and had little energy to do anything. He certainly couldn't continue doing our sideline business.

The week he received his SSDI notification, he shared how much better he felt contributing to our finances again. Things seemed to be looking up.

I had been in this position for four years when the economy crashed. Just as I returned from my mother's funeral, the owners told me they had sold the business. I loved my job and looked forward to helping the new owner as the company entered a new phase. But then it happened again!

The new owner didn't like the fact that I wasn't bringing in enough new clients, so he put me on ninety days probation. When the ninety days came and went, with no real increase of clients and no termination mentioned, I cautiously moved forward. But I knew my days were numbered.

In an attempt to be free of this newly stressful employment situation, I began another job search. The economy was still in recovery and I was unable to find new options for my chosen career within the senior industry, so I put all my energies into attempting to grow the business.

Each day I'd pray, "Just stay with me, Lord, when I falter, feel weak, confused, attacked, and don't know the direction I must go. For now, I will stay the course and be open to your direction and answers. Praise you, Lord. This day is yours!"

Other days I added the words of Psalm 20:4 to my prayer, seeking the desires of my heart and God's ability to make my plans succeed. I would pray, "I don't quite see my direction yet, I need you to clarify it. I need to use the talents you've given me. Help me to find proper direction for my days and for my life."

Since the new owner wasn't pleased with my performance but I still had the job, some days I would pray that God would just break the yoke off my neck (Jeremiah 30:8) and have him fire me!

The stress was sometimes unbearable and I felt like David struggling to keep going. I would rise early every day and stay up late, trying to work for a solution, but all in vain (Psalm 127:2).

I knew the job was destined to end. I just didn't know when. But I had learned to rely on the Lord's direction as Paul did (1 Corinthians 16:7). The end, the new beginning, would happen only if and when the Lord would permit it.

I decided to ride it all the way out until the new owner told me to leave. I wanted to be out of there. I needed a break, but I wasn't a quitter!

Once more I prayed, "Help me, Lord, to test my actions (Galatians 6:4) and give me the proper direction."

I chose not to compromise in any way and the job lasted another seven months with the new owner.

Finally, the Lord, who was the *only* one guiding my career, chose to have me leave that job without another to replace it—to take me out of it completely. I was terminated the day before I was to go on vacation. But I learned another valuable lesson—God would *never* abandon me.

Once again Cal reassured me God would take care of us. My Jewish, non-religious husband actually seemed more connected to God's will at this moment than I did! So, armed with his encouragement, I was able to start another business of my own. This new venture allowed me to remain in ministry to seniors and their families. God honored my passion to help these people and the decision became the bridge that brought in income until I moved into full-time work with a hospice company started by a friend as the director of volunteers.

Things were going well with my friend's company, but something was becoming very wrong with our friendship and my position in her company. Things had been great between us for so long. I learned so much from her and she thought I was doing a great job. But I was also balancing a dual role as friend and employee. As a manager, all I wanted to do was create the best department I could. However, through a serious misunderstanding, I was forced to resign a week before I could finalize hiring details with a competitor company.

As stressful and difficult as this job separation was, including the loss of a fourteen-year friendship, I clearly saw the hand of God throughout the entire job search initiation, interview process, and final move to the new hospice company. I knew God's timing was perfect, but most importantly, I finally saw the old job as "just a job." It no longer held idol status in my life where most of my other work experiences had. I also began to understand Cal's job loss pain. It helped me more compassionately understand how hard things must have been for him over the years. What a breakthrough! I prayed, "Oh, Lord, please don't let me go back there ever again!"

Because of the hurt I felt in the way my friend forced me to resign, I came to the awareness that working for that company had just been a job. I also saw God's hand clearly as I worked hard to forgive my friend and move on. Within a short couple of weeks, I was hired by the new hospice company where I would work until retirement.

Who would have known that a job or a business could actually become an idol? Of course, I would never worship in front of a wooden statue or some hunk of stone and expect it to help me, but what is God's definition of an idol? What does he consider "other gods"?

His first commandment is pretty clear:

"You shall have no other gods before me." (Exodus 20:3)

Worshiping a job or my own business and seeing it as the be all and end all of my life was clearly a violation of God's first commandment. Over the years these workaholic business idols had become harmful to my relationship to God and to my marriage.

One Sunday at The Shoreline Church, the pastor said, "An idol is something that's created and put into a place where your heart puts it as an ultimate thing. When a good thing becomes an ultimate thing (becomes the only thing) in our lives…this is an idol! But we must center our lives on him!"

Work and career have often been idols throughout my life. It was a constant battle of priorities.

THE HEART OF MY PERSONAL STRUGGLE

Seeing any job as the answer to our need for security, my need to feel important (pride), and an opportunity to make a difference in the world seemed as if I sometimes gave it too much importance by relying on my career for my identity rather than relying on God.

I think I knew this truth all along, but it took this newest dramatic set of events at my friend's company to finally show me how God had led me away from a toxic environment into a regular job with its purpose only to provide income for us.

Of course, I would do my best in the position, but not for any glory or praise directed toward me. I knew this job was clearly a God-thing and he deserved the glory for bringing it to me.

I prayed, "Oh, Lord, don't ever let me forget how clear you were in guiding me through this process. Even as I sometimes lost faith in the weeks between the resignation and the new job offer, you understood and took me through it."

When each of these job separation processes began, I was always so sure I would soon feel better. Finally, *some* action had been taken and this job instability would soon be over.

How wrong I was! Somehow each time things just seemed to get worse. Apparently I had the same lesson to learn that Peter did when Jesus filled his boat with fish (John 21:3–6). We can only be truly successful, even in those things we are naturally talented to do, when we follow the Lord in his strength, wisdom, and guidance.

Each failed job experience prepared me to learn from the Lord, to trust him more, and let him guide me toward his true will for my life. One of my biggest lessons continues to be that I constantly need to "die to self." This lesson became a personal transformation from death to life and I was doing it on behalf of others as well as myself.

> "Then he said to them all: 'Whoever wants to be my disciple must deny themselves and take up their cross daily and follow me.'" (Luke 9:23)

This has not been an easy road! But it was the much-needed lesson I had to learn as I journeyed forward with my husband and kept jobs in their proper place.

I never grieved about my days of trials (and more were to come) because they had successfully taken me from being just a believer in Christ to becoming a follower of him. As James puts it:

> "Consider it pure joy, my brothers and sisters, whenever you face trials of many kinds, because you know that the testing of your faith develops perseverance. Let perseverance finish its work so that you may be mature and complete, not lacking anything." (James 1:2–4)

I wouldn't be here today to share my story unless the Lord had changed me and put me in a new place … his place.

> "Wait for the Lord; be strong and take heart and wait for the Lord." (Psalm 27:14)

I praise God for his guidance through my ongoing struggle to keep proper balance in the priorities of my life. Each time God forgave me and I was given new opportunities to re-evaluate my motivations. Original goals returned to my marriage. I stopped neglecting God as I had before. A reborn focus immerged, which reinforced my relationship with God and created a loving relationship with the husband I adored—to be there for our children and their families, and to become the loving, nurturing wife, mother, and grandmother God had always intended me to be. These things needed to come before my church activities or my career. What could be more important? I thought that I'd finally put the control of my life back where it belongs—in God's hands.

But wait. Have I really given God the complete control? Probably not—this is my ongoing, life-long personal struggle.

Every day I must remind myself of what it says in John:

> "Very truly I tell you, unless a kernel of wheat falls to the ground and dies, it remains only a single seed. But if it dies, it produces many seeds." (John 12:24-26)

Jesus uses the symbol of the kernel of wheat to demonstrate that when it falls to the ground and dies, a new plant is created. This shows the importance of dying to self or dying to your ego in order to produce godly fruit in your life.

As painful as it is, I must still work to die to my "self" daily!

Chapter Wrap-Up:

In what ways do you struggle to let go and deny yourself for the benefit of others?

What priorities do you struggle with to find balance in your life?

Describe a time that you have tried to determine your own future without consulting God?

What was the outcome?

Have you been operating in your own strength or in God's?

What bad habits do you think God is trying to break out of you?

What steps can you take to grow closer to God and let yourself be pruned?

Chapter 8

Losing Self

During the early years of my marriage, society was changing dramatically. Women had choices between careers and families or they could do both. Women's Liberation was growing stronger and stronger. Housewives and mothers had identity issues that I easily fell into. They were not respected and, unless a woman knew the Lord, they often missed the importance of both roles to the family. I started my marriage at twenty, began motherhood and my career almost simultaneously at twenty-three. Given my family background of always feeling not good enough, I soon identified that my career was where I could achieve the most recognition and acceptance to prove I was, indeed, good enough.

That's the problem I had when I became a mother. I think that's why I kept searching for fulfillment in the workplace. The workplace seemed to be an easy place to excel and find success that overcame the not good enough syndrome. I had such a desperate need to be important in this world. John and Stasi Eldredge in their book, *Captivating: Unveiling the Mystery of a Woman's Soul* agree, concluding that a woman's heart longs "… for three things: to be romanced, to play an irreplaceable role in a great adventure, and to unveil beauty. That's what makes a woman come alive." And "A woman knows, down in her soul, that she longs to bring beauty to the world … This is in her heart, part of her design."[1]

It is important for us to find our place in the world.

I find it extremely unfortunate that, at one time, I was unable to acknowledge the importance of training our children to be the best that they could be even though it was God's goal for that time in my life. Taking delight in my children was often difficult. Sometimes I felt like God was raising my children without much help from me. I was failing to bring beauty to the world through my own motherhood.

Why, oh why, Lord was I never happy where you put me? Thank you, Lord, for eventually bringing my focus back home for our great kids! You protected them so often from the potential destruction my selfish efforts toward self-fulfillment could have wrought upon their precious lives.

Successful raising of children requires both mothers and fathers, but I wasn't always the mother God intended. I was often way too selfish.

So, back when we were raising our kids, in my own quest to be self-important in the world, I had clearly lost focus on how important raising our children and being a wife to Cal really was. Never quite measuring up placed within me a strong drive to accomplish, to achieve, and to be important. Coupled with the world's very strong message to women that housewives and mothers have little significance, I easily fell into the enemy's trap. By the world's standards, housewives and mothers are often seen as little more than maids and babysitters. But that's *not* what God thinks! In reality, wives and mothers are responsible for raising the next generation of the world's leaders.

It wasn't until the Lord came into my life at thirty-two that I began to learn the truth. I'm afraid, however, that the world's ways stayed with me for way too long before I realized I had some personality pruning to do in my life.

Battling with my self, my pride, and competing with Cal have been lifelong struggles for me. Challenges within my career have often been caused by my selfish, prideful behavior and a reliance on those jobs for fulfillment instead of relying on God.

Coupled with my need to compete with Cal to be as important as he was to our family and in the world, our marriage and family were at risk. If I didn't make some very necessary changes through Holy Spirit guidance, we would be in trouble. But it has not been easy.

When your self is dying it hurts a whole lot! We are just like jars of clay—very, very fragile. Jesus can put our pieces back together, but it means surrendering to his will.

A pastor recently said, "Surrender generally means to declare yourself defeated—giving up control and giving up the fight." This is certainly true if we take God out of the equation and try to do things ourselves. Then, we are quickly defeated. But as the pastor shared, "If we allow God to take control, we are victorious!"

Ephesians 4:22 tells us we are "… taught, with regard to your former way of life, to put off your old self." But I still have a very strong, old self, which can be "corrupted by deceitful desires." Even in retirement my own (desperate) prayer continues to be, "Help me, Lord, not to continue to be deceived, but to be led by the Holy Spirit in everything I do!"

I must confess I recently made a big mistake, though I kept praying for Holy Spirit guidance and searched the Word for answers. I wasn't patient and I ended up choosing my own way anyway. Oh, the Lord has forgiven me, but my way, as opposed to following the Holy Spirit, led to a chain of events, which I wish I'd been able to stop. I can't share the details, as other people were involved, but suffice it to say, even as an older woman, my sinful nature is always just below the surface. So, I continue to call on God's promises to keep my human nature in check. "And the God of all grace, who called you to his eternal glory in Christ, after you have suffered a little while, will himself restore you and make you strong, firm, and steadfast" (1 Peter 5:10 NIV). I regret that others were hurt by my failure to obey God. I have asked for God's forgiveness and the forgiveness of others, but I am still working to forgive myself. I need to fully realize that Jesus has already paid the full ransom for my disobedience and I need to let it go.

So, I "suffered for a while," but now I pray daily to remain "strong, firm and steadfast" and proceed only in God's ways!

God reminded me this is an ongoing struggle and is a spiritual battle. This is not a battle against flesh and blood. It is a battle against the "powers of this dark world and against the spiritual forces of evil in the heavenly realms" (Ephesians 6:12 NIV). I have an enemy who wants "to steal and kill and destroy" (John 10:10 NIV), but the best news ever is that Jesus has come that I may have life—a full life. I can be victorious in the battle with Jesus at my side. I was finally ready to fight back to recovery with the strength of the Holy Spirit behind me and protected by the armor of God (See Ephesians 6:10–18). I can overcome the darts of the enemy even when I stumble.

Chapter Wrap-Up:

Describe a time you sought God's Holy Spirit for guidance.

Describe a time, when you got ahead of the Lord and had to ask for forgiveness.

Would you call yourself selfish or generous? Why?

Chapter 9

The Wise Woman Builds Her House

"Nevertheless, in the Lord woman is not independent of man, nor is man independent of woman." (1 Corinthians 11:11)

Gary Thomas states in *Sacred Influence* that, "…if your husband is spiritually weaker than you are, your job is to bear with his failings in such a way that you build him up, not tear him down. Instead of assuming the worst, call him to his best. Some women, rather than building up their spiritually weaker husbands, expend their verbal energy discouraging their husbands and tearing them down, berating them for their perceived lack of spiritual leadership."[1]

Unfortunately, I had been a verbally discouraging wife for many years.

Anabel Gillham explains in *The Confident Woman: Knowing Who You Are in Christ* that "God created man, woman and marriage. Marriage: A male and a female, entirely unique, agreeing to join themselves together with vows of love, commitment and trust; two facing life as one, realizing that love will not hold their marriage together, but that their marriage will hold their love together, acknowledging each other's imperfections but accepting each other nonetheless…"[2]

All wives (and especially mothers) need help. The very first place we should look for that help is in our Lord. We have God's support, but we also need to gain our husband's support in the struggle to survive as wives. This is especially critical during early motherhood when the children are young. Wives need to depend upon both God and their husbands. God provides husbands to help their wives as partners. In no way was marriage ever meant to be one sided. Marriage is a partnership and marriage takes work. The work starts with a closer walk with God.

Betty Coble in her book *Woman—Aware and Choosing*, reminds us that, "trying to live out (our lives) by someone else's vague definition" of what a wife is can create an identity crisis within us. Coble continues, "Part of the problem in defining roles and finding identity is in the area of fear about not being as important as the other person in the marriage."[3]

Never quite measuring up in my own home of origin caused me to seek fulfillment in the workplace rather than in the home. The Eldredge's chapter on "Wounded Femininity" explains many things to me.

Growing up, I was exposed to considerable shame. For example, I'd proudly bring home a "B" in a tough class only to be confronted with my mother's statements like, "Why wasn't it an A?" I can still hear her saying, "You're just not living up to your potential."

I felt so defeated. All the joy of not getting a "C" was for naught. Why couldn't I ever please my mother?

Even in art classes, where I maybe had some natural talent, the not being good enough feelings crept in to destroy my enthusiasm and motivation. I once created a picture that my art teacher loved. But, because it was supposed to be a picture of the forest in Fall, I thought it was bad. I had made a mistake on it, so I added gray for some smoke and turned it into a forest fire instead. It won an award, but in my mind it wasn't perfect so it wasn't good enough.

This just confirmed that I wasn't good enough and that there was something wrong with me. My award-winning picture became an ugly reminder of my inadequacies.

Today, I know my mom was just doing what she felt was best. But those rejections hurt. They hurt so much I finally decided I just didn't care. Actually, I did care, but not because it was important to my mother. I had to wait until I was ready to be self-motivated. Self-motivation placed a certain drive within me and, if taken in balance, that was a good thing. Self-motivation allowed me to go back to college and finally get my BA in psychology with a three-year-old and a new baby in tow. But often the balance of being so self-motivated was off.

My competitive nature and workaholic drive often caused my work life balance to get off kilter and my childhood issues of never being good enough led to compensating behaviors throughout my adult life.

Though my family of origin provided well economically and socially for my two brothers and me, there was something missing emotionally. To keep up the proper social face, my parents never fought or argued in public or in private. They appeared perfect. I believe this is why I was drawn to the emotional outbursts that Cal's family was so prone to have. His mother had quite a temper and, when we were dating, she wasn't embarrassed to be herself in front of me. I welcomed that level of honest expression of feelings.

Families are supposed to provide love and examples of healthy relationships. My family was dysfunctional and failed to meet the relational needs of my brothers and me. We were not permitted to express negative emotions. One brother learned to stuff his anger and I learned to let it just explode.

Somehow, I think some of my lack of humility was because these relational needs failed to be met. This created an intense need in me to prove my worth.

Praise God, gradually Christ-likeness has worked itself into me through circumstances that brought humility into my life and Christ-likeness is certainly great gain!

Rather than being a good little girl and behaving myself so I would appear to be socially acceptable like my parents, I learned it was okay to be me. Our move to California early in our marriage allowed me to discover who I was without the judgment of my mother. Cal always accepted me and my many faults. A pastor once shared in a sermon that God doesn't reject us. So, where I felt rejected by my parents, I was accepted by my husband and by God. What a blessing!

Often my journey has been one of hurt due to not feeling good enough. I learned that on the one hand we are never going to be good enough, but that Christ came to make us good enough through being a Christ-follower. (Romans 8:1)

Wow! I can be good enough—even for God!

I certainly never felt that kind of acceptance as a child. Clearly, a big key for my growth has involved the grace of God who drew me to himself.

Given the hurtful issues feeling inadequate caused me, I am thankful that somehow we were able to raise our daughter, Julie, to be her own person. Cal and I gave her all of our wisdom and have watched where she has developed from there. Hopefully, she never felt as if she wasn't good enough and I was careful not to raise her to be a clone of me. What a joy it is to see where the Lord has taken her and her brothers in life.

My ego strives to help me prevent failure in the eyes of man—that not being good enough thing again!

Pastor Seth Ebel's *Faith That Follows: Experiencing Discipleship to Jesus* taught me to be on my guard in the area of our "functional saviors." Functional saviors are good things, but they are without Jesus in the center of them. They can become the source of our identity, security, and significance because we hold an adulterous admiration for them.[4]

For me, this seemed to clearly relate to those insecurities caused by my issues of not being good enough.

All my business endeavors may well have served as functional saviors throughout my life—it has been my identity, my security, and my significance. As I reviewed my own job-related hurts and pains, I began to better understand Cal's pain during his unemployment. I only wish I'd had these experiences earlier so I could have been more compassionate, patient, and sympathetic toward him when he was hurting. Understanding this in these terms has helped me to know what needed to change. Lord, please help me always to put you in the center of all I do! Not my jobs or my self.

Until I read Linda Dillow's *Creative Counterpart: Becoming the Woman, Wife, and Mother You Have Longed To Be*, I had missed another important truth. Dillow explains three marital plans, including that of Creative Counterpart, "a helpmate, a compliment to her husband ... the Executive Vice President." Within our family structure, I had actually been Cal's Executive Vice President.[5] What a wonderful concept! Obviously, this author was talking my language in allowing me to have *some* prideful ego!

In *Sacred Influence*, author Gary Thomas says, "Women are not told to sit on the sidelines and cheer for their husbands as the men run the show. On the contrary, from the very beginning women share God's command for humans to rule, subdue and manage this earth. They are co-regents."[6]

Our family, like any business, needed a leader. But the leader also needed a right-hand assistant.

I discovered I could accept being the Executive VP. That was cool! "The *wife* is to be a *participating follower* knowing that she is obedient to God when she is following her husband."[7]

As long as I was in the respected role of Executive VP, I knew I could survive. Our life became so much more peaceful during those times when I operated within this mindset. But when I forgot and started taking over as President or CEO, things went awry. For a very long time, this balance was a constant and continuing struggle for me.

I had no idea how strong I still was in my self, until I truly tried to react by doing nothing!

Though I had always paid the bills, Cal once decided he had a better way. I tried to release the task to him, but couldn't easily let go and trust the process or trust God! Unnecessary stress ensued as I fought the idea instead of letting him try his.

"Marriage is one of the Lord's faithful tools used to battle our pride as well as teach us about Christ's love for his church. There is life and victory in marriage but it only comes through humble love, sacrifice, and a steady commitment to live as one."[8]

As I was learning to become the Executive VP of our family, the Lord was showing me my sinful, critical nature toward Cal on almost everything he did, especially during his periods of unemployment. Later, I worried I would be unable to restore Cal to his former greatness as President/CEO of our family after I had inflicted so much harm.

Thank you, Lord, for reminding me during this time that "with man this is impossible, but not with God; all things are possible with God" (Mark 10:27). And thank you for giving me a new concept of the role our careers should serve. And, more importantly, how transient they can be.

I had the promise that, just as the Lord had protected and guided our kids, he would do the same for Cal.

"It doesn't say wives should respect *perfect* husbands or even *godly* husbands. It says that husbands — no qualifier — should be respected." Cal, because he was a husband, deserved respect. I might have disagreed with his judgment. I might have objected to the way he handled things, but according to the Bible, his position alone called me to give him proper respect. If I withheld this respect, Cal sometimes stopped hearing me.[9]

I had so much trouble yielding to Cal with respect when he was not working, when he was a different person, and when I felt I had to take control. I just did not respect him! But as Thomas explains, men "desperately want their wives' affirmation."[10] This was so hard for us back then!

"Affirmation is more than a man's desire—much more. Acceptance and encouragement are biblical requirements. (see Romans 15:7, 1 Thessalonians 5:11, Hebrews 3:13). Your first step—the primary one—is to love, accept, and even honor your imperfect husband."[11]

Thomas explains, "Guys rise to praise. When someone compliments us, we want to keep that person's positive opinion intact. We love how it feels when our wives respect us; we get a rush like nothing else when we hear her praise or see that look of awe in her eyes–and we will all but travel the ends of the earth to keep it coming."[12]

Clearly, I had to learn to see Cal differently. I needed to learn how to love Cal *as he was*. It was not always easy!

As Thomas states, "marriage has to be built stone by stone. We have to make deliberate choices; we have to be active and confront the weaknesses we see in ourselves and in each other." God "allows us to face issues that may terrify us and make us feel completely inadequate—he may even walk us through our deepest fears—so that we can grow in him. The Bible is adamant about this. Spiritual growth takes place by persevering through difficult times."[13]

Consider these Scripture passages below. There is the assumption the husband that Thomas is referring to is a believer, though this does not imply that the believer is to be any less willing to yield to her unbelieving husband.

> "For the unbelieving husband has been sanctified through his wife, and the unbelieving wife has been sanctified through her believing husband." (1 Corinthians 7:14)

As the wife of an unbeliever, I always surrounded myself with godly men: pastors, friends, and a son to whom I could go to with questions of submission. If your husband doesn't know the Lord, I recommend you find godly men and women to provide the guidance and support you will need.

However, if your husband is physically or emotionally abusive (believer or not), he is not living up to what Scripture commands.

> "A good tree cannot bear bad fruit, and a bad tree cannot bear good fruit. Every tree that does not bear good fruit is cut down and thrown into the fire. Thus, by their fruit you will recognize them." (Matthew 7:18–20)

Your husband's fruit will be evident. If you are in an abusive relationship, you need to pray for the Lord's divine wisdom in following your husband's lead. You need wise counsel from friends, professionals, and clergy who are solid followers of Christ. Don't walk your walk alone and don't be foolish. God will guide you as you seek his will for your life. Abusive relationships are in a totally different category when it comes to submission. If you are involved in this kind of relationship, please talk to a professional. Go to your pastor. Get some sort of help.

The Lord gave me many Scriptures relating to our position in the world and I had to heed each one, remembering that

> "the wisdom of this world is foolishness in God's sight." (1 Corinthians 3:19a)

God had placed us in his loving hands.

> "If you belonged to the world, it would love you as its own. As it is, you do not belong to the world, but I have chosen you out of the world. That is why the world hates you." (John 15:19)

Paul shared his heart with the people of Corinth when he said, "I beg you that when I come I may not have to be as bold as I expect to be toward some people who think that we live by the standards of this world" (2 Corinthians 10:2).

This reminded me again, not to "love the world or anything in the world. If anyone loves the world, love for the Father is not in them. For everything in the world—the lust of the flesh, the lust of the eyes, and the pride of life—comes not from the Father but from the world. The world and its desires pass away, but whoever does the will of God lives forever (1 John 2:15–17).

God has created man and woman to be helpmates (soul mates) to work together as a successful team for him—to complement each other. God said, "It is not good for the man to be alone. I will make a helper suitable for him" (Genesis 2:18).

God didn't say, "I will make a destroyer for him!"

I was created to be Cal's supporter, not his keeper. God told us that we are to "Submit (yield) to one another out of reverence for Christ" (Ephesians 5:21, addition mine).

During the difficult periods there was often a lot of blaming going on. You may think that your husband has some lesson to learn when you experience a lack of blessing in a situation, but be careful. It could be, as it has been in my own life, that the blamer has just as big, if not a bigger lesson to learn. Remember the question posed in the Word?

> "Why do you look at the speck of sawdust in your brother's eye and pay no attention to the plank in your own eye?" (Matthew 7:3)

We all have planks in our own eyes!

I also learned many years ago that changing Cal was not my job. The only one I can change is myself. However, in changing myself I often did experience an accompanying change in Cal. Ruth Graham once said of her husband, Billy Graham, "It's my job to love and respect Billy. It's God's job to make him good."

Once at Women's Bible Study one of the women shared that she compliments her husband even when he isn't acting the desired way or having a desired reaction. She chooses to see him in a positive way—the way she wanted him to be. By accepting him, he was subtly being changed and living up to the reputation she was creating for him. So, by changing the things she could change (her attitude), he was reacting to her in a new way. This, then, resulted in change.

Word of advice: don't try to change your guy! It will never happen! Prayer is the only way, but even prayer can lead to a wrong attitude in a wife. Pray for your husbands, but leave it *all* up to God—his annoying habits, gross actions, etc. Leave it alone and change *your* own attitudes toward your husband instead. Learn to accept yourself, as well. I discovered that I wasn't perfect, I just did my best. I asked God to change me in important areas and I learned to relax. I should share here that almost every time Cal needed change in my eyes, it was ME who became changed the most. God obviously had areas to work on in my life and used Cal's circumstances to change me.

Rather than trying to change our men, I believe we must do whatever we can to understand them. Understanding and acceptance is an important thing in any relationship. In her book, *Woman, Aware and Choosing*, Coble says, "Building a life together requires knowing who you are as a wife and understanding who he is as a husband." She goes on to say, "A wife needs to keep her eyes open to discover who her husband has become each day, so she will keep up with the relationship." [14]

My journey in obedient surrender took me to a deeper place of understanding and acceptance of my husband and who he was. In his book *Emotionally Healthy Spirituality Day by Day: A 40-Day Journey with the Daily Office*, author Peter Scazzero says, "Journeys involve movement, action, stops and starts, detours, delays and trips into the unknown."[15] That has certainly been true for my journey through life.

Chapter Wrap-Up:

What is your definition of marriage?

In what ways do you struggle with your role as a wife?

Are you happy in your place as a wife and mother? Why or why not?

What are some functional saviors in your life?

Chapter 10

Stop Being Superwoman and Start Being Faithful

Back in 1975 when Coble wrote *Woman—Aware and Choosing*, she saw the emerging rebellion in which women were engaged. Sometimes I, too, seriously questioned God's wisdom in placing men as "head, protector, controller, director, manager, commander-in-chief, or whatever you choose to call him, over woman." That societal rebellion has never gone away.

I eventually recognized the wisdom of having the protection of a male head as I spoke with single mothers who struggled daily to determine and then do God's will within their families by themselves. But this feminine rebellion has grown to a point where many of the world's women require no commitment from their men. They simply live together. There is no respect given to the man for his place in making family decisions. Strong women libbers declare they don't need the inept, helpless creatures. Media advertising sometimes advances these beliefs by showing men as pretty stupid beings. Sure, it makes funny commercials, but it's a terrible example for our kids. Kids are growing up with these worldly examples regardless of how they are trained at home (unless, perhaps, you throw out the TV and home school them.)

The removal of the husband and father from our households has been devastating to our society. I had always blamed the woman's movement for weakening fatherhood in our nation. However, research done by David Blankenhorn for his book *Fatherless America: Confronting Our Most Urgent Social Problem* discovered that in 1943, during WWII, was when this devastating change began. Back then, the Selective Service needed more troops. So, amid tremendous public outcry, fathers began leaving behind wives and children to fight the war. This caused a massive deficiency of male role modeling in the lives of their growing children, especially when husbands failed to return home. [1]

Also, during this time, by necessity, women discovered the workplace and began supporting themselves independent of their husbands. Even my own mother, trained as a teacher, worked at an aircraft plant prior to her marriage to my father after WWII. Mom was an accomplished woman who obtained a Master's degree at a time when most women did not even go to college. Her art background enabled her to read blueprints for aircraft design.

I believe that many of the women forced to work in non-traditional female jobs during WWII may have eventually contributed to the downfall of the family also. Though marriages didn't begin tumbling through divorce until the sixties, I believe when our society gave women a taste of "the other side" that desire was created within them to enter the workplace.

By creating a desire in women to enter the more exciting workplace, women were being lured away from their homes. Even those who did not leave to enter the workplace began to encourage their daughters (my generation) to aspire to greater heights than their mothers had been permitted to. Since then, we have been told we can have it all—career, marriage, kids. We could be Superwoman!

Total Truth: Liberating Christianity from Its Cultural Captivity by Nancy Pearcey explains that women "may not have much control in the private sphere (the home) until they have children, which can be a difficult and even traumatic transition."

Yes, that was my journey!

Pearcey goes on to share, "It struck me as decidedly unfair that women should experience such intense pressure to choose between the two major tasks of adult life between pursuing a calling and raising the next generation. Our identity and self-worth have been built primarily on our public persona and accomplishments especially at work." [2]

Yes … staying at home only raising kids was just not me.

But in *Woman—Aware and Choosing,* Coble makes a good point in the area of priorities. She says it is crucial to remember that "children are in the home on a temporary basis. They are there to be loved, trained and enjoyed."[3]

That's why Coble and I agree that our number one job as parents is to raise independent children. They need to learn they have a place in your life, but so does their daddy.

One of the saddest things I've seen are parents that put everything into their children and they feel alone and disconnected when the children grow up and leave home. Often these empty nesters find they have nothing left but themselves and, because they never got to know one another, they actually have nothing! The children were their entire lives.

Cal and I didn't have that problem. I think the greatest day in our life came when our youngest, Timmy, stopped holding my hand, so I could hold Cal's again. And as the kids left the nest, we were finally able to enjoy being truly alone—together! When we wanted a kid around we could borrow a grandchild or two. We loved the balance between date nights and babysitting.

Coble points out that putting Daddy first is actually healthier for the children. "When a child is in control, he will always be the center of attention and very insecure. If a mother really loves her children, she will discipline (teach and train) them to see how valuable the husband/wife relationship is to her."[4]

In *Creative Counterpart*, Dillow offers a great explanation of God's priorities. Keeping things in order makes life easier to live. God must be first in our priorities, then our husbands, then our children, then our home, then our self before *anything* outside our homes.[5]

Boy, did I have it mixed up! My self and my activities outside the home were so often my first priorities. When the Lord entered my life, I knew he needed to have a place, but only *sometimes* did I make him priority number one! Then there were days when I knew my kids were the most important, but where was poor Cal?

Often he was last, because, after all, he was an adult. He couldn't possibly have any needs. How wrong I was! Though it was still a struggle, priorities began to become much clearer. Getting up to study the Word and pray first thing each morning put God first in my life.

A friend suggested an excellent thing for me to work on—being quiet and waiting on the Lord. Much easier said than done for me, but relaxation would allow me to take more time with the Lord in his Word and prayer.

I started with Millie Stamm's daily meditation books.

One morning I stopped at the beach after driving the kids to school. I meditated, read, prayed, and just stayed quiet for several minutes. This was such a difficult thing for me to do. I'm more of a Martha than a Mary (Luke 10:38–42). The day was a busy one. I had so much to do that I really had no time to stop for God time. But I needed God's help, so I pushed through. I eventually began trying harder to be attentive to Cal and seek him out to make a connection. As the kids left to be on their own, I made myself as available as needed for Cal, which was sometimes more often than I had expected, especially as his health deteriorated.

As the Lord granted me a few speaking engagements and other fun things, I knew I would be tempted away from time with Cal and the kids. Praise God I eventually started to maintain a proper balance and follow in God's perfect timing through my life through constant prayer and daily digging into his Word.

As the Lord opened an opportunity, I would carefully pray before taking action. I realized that patiently waiting for the Holy Spirit was far more productive. I began following the Lord instead of taking control myself. Wow! I was becoming a Christ-*follower*.

In *Sacred Influence*, Gary Thomas said, "We live in a culture that glorifies selfishness more than responsibility. Books and movies urge us to 'follow our hearts,' regardless of our commitments. We need to recapture the beauty of responsibility and the glory of faithfulness. A supermodel peaks in her early twenties, while the beauty of a godly, responsible woman grows with each decade. Some women try in vain to preserve a fading past, while others experience the joy of forging a new future. It all depends on what they value the most. Families crumble because we've lost respect for responsibility."[6]

I praise God, that he entered my life when he did and has continued to guide my life choices in a magnificent way, which preserved my marriage!

Chapter Wrap-Up:

Name two ways you struggle with society's belief about the role you have as wife or mother.

What are your thoughts about fatherhood and your husband's success or failure as a father?

How can you strive to keep God number one in your life—even above your family?

Chapter 11

Submission

As I began to understand my role more as a wife and mother, using God's model, I began to venture into another difficult area: submission.

> "Wives, submit yourselves to your own husbands as you do to the Lord. For the husband is the head of the wife as Christ is the head of the church, his body, of which he is the Savior." (Ephesians 5:22–33)

I had heard a pastor once explain submission as "yielding." That is so much easier to understand, don't you think? We all yield in life—to police officers, our bosses, traffic lights, etc.

For wives, our culture has messed up the word submission to make it what it was not intended to be. John Stott states in *The Message of Ephesians (The Bible Speaks Today Series)*, "There is nothing demeaning about this, for her submission is not to be unthinking obedience to his rule but rather grateful acceptance of his care."[1]

There is a proper attitude for the wife to yield in submission. Her attitude is not to be a passive, disengaged, cowering one, but to be a Spirit-filled, joyful, willing one and act as Jesus had done. Nor should she have the resentful attitude I sometimes exhibited.

There were days when I would dedicate myself to being the perfect little submissive wife. But even in that description, the truth lay just below the surface. "Perfect little submissive wife" connotes a lack of respect, on my part, for that woman. Until I was *completely* controlled by the Spirit, this would remain a struggle.

Jesus is our model of submission—to the law and to the Father. He learned obedience to his brothers, his death on the cross, his suffering, etc. These acts of obedience become his model of submission to us.

This all sounds well and good, but when the rubber hits the road, I had so much to learn about submitting, even if it can actually be called yielding!

Learning to yield can be fulfilling as a Spirit-filled, Christ-like, equality-maintained role within the body of Christ for the glory of God. But this has always been such a hard lesson for me to learn, as you will see.

I have discovered that, often, we find ourselves in prisons of our own making because we sinfully attempt to take control of our own lives instead of yielding to the Lord. However, as the Lord Jesus led his apostles out of jail (Acts 5:19–20), he has led me, too, from my prison.

When God allows the enemy to put us into a prison—when we are at our wits end–the Holy Spirit gives us direction and the anointing to be freed. The Lord had allowed me to be imprisoned to demonstrate his love for me, so I could experience his freedom. He also locked me out, unable to enter that prison again. My personal prison was the bondage of self-control (as opposed to God-control). Over time, I haven't tried to re-enter that prison—too often! At times my prideful, workaholic tendencies, selfishness, and competitive nature have headed me back toward that prison. Just in time, I remember the Lord Jesus Christ, who has truly set me free from these destructive behaviors! In all of this I must remember that it is he who gives me peace, not my circumstances.

I prayed for forgiveness and help to release those behaviors and my desire to control, so I could yield to Cal regardless of my circumstances. As I apologized to Cal, my desire to control lessoned.

The act of yielding has different meanings for each individual couple. God does not make duplicates. I can only share my story. What has worked for us might not work the same way for another couple. What I understood for sure was that wifely submission to Cal was *absolutely necessary* for us to achieve the satisfying, successful relationship we finally did achieve. It goes far beyond our own relationship. Our children were ever watching, ever-absorbing. We were setting examples for them in our acts of yielding to one another. When I was disrespectful and rebellious toward Cal's leadership, how could I possibly expect our children to be any different? I needed to have a yielding spirit not only for us but for our children, as well. They learned from my yielding to Cal and to God by what they saw at home.

"(God) instructed man to be the leader; woman to complete, complement, and follow; children to be trained, enjoyed, and sent out from home." You've heard it before: The best gift we can give to our children is to love their father and vice versa. Loving also means accepting. "The day a wife accepts the fact that she is not responsible for her husband's actions is one of the greatest days of her life...The wife is not responsible for the husband side of the marriage, *but* she is responsible for *all* of the *wife* side of marriage. Children do not need two mothers. They need a mother and a father."[2]

I was called to "love" Cal and I believe that meant putting an "L" into the word "compete." I was competing with Cal, but the Lord was calling me to walk beside him, to complete him. As his wife, I had to watch my attitude, as well as my words. Cal wasn't always right, but when I non-judgmentally, gently shared my opinions, he would usually listen. If, on the other hand, I argued strongly or tried to manipulate him into my way of thinking, Cal would cease to hear me and just begin doing whatever he wanted to do in the first place. This was not communication! This was not completing. This was attempting to be right, to be the leader. There can only be *one* leader, so I finally figured I might as well get with God's program!

I had never stopped to think that every time I criticized, manipulated, rebuked, or defied Cal, I was doing just what Delilah did when she cut off Samson's hair (Judges 16). Each time I acted in this way, I removed a little more of Cal's strength as family leader.

Though Delilah had evil intentions and I did not, the outcome was the same. If I manipulated to get my own way, dished out hurtful criticism, constantly rebuked Cal (making him feel like a little boy), or generally failed to yield to my husband as to the Lord (Ephesians 5:23), I was just like Delilah. Cal's manhood was being destroyed, a little at a time with all the hurtful things I did and said. As I discovered the evil within my self, I prayed that the Lord would repair Cal's manhood to its former strength.

Every time I complimented Cal, worked by his side as a teammate, was honest in communicating my needs, and avoided treating him like a bad little boy, I was able to see the strength of a man in him. He exhibited the strength God had called him to in leading our family—whether he had a personal relationship with the Lord or not. He needed my help just the way I needed his. Finally, I decided to be there for him.

Strong Christian families are built through men who have become strong followers of Christ. As women, we have the power to strengthen our men or take their strength away.

Remember Sarai, Abram's wife? When her husband announced that the Lord had told him to pack up everything and take off for parts unknown what do you think her reaction was? I know what mine might have been! Even with my natural risk-taking personality, I need a little more security than that. I would need certain questions answered before we set out on such a journey. I like things ordered and I don't like change! However, had Sarai not obeyed her husband, she might never have received the blessing of her own long-awaited child.

Chapter Wrap-Up:

What prisons of your own making are you trapped in?

How could you be free from these prisons?

How do you submit or yield to your husband?

Do you manipulate to get your way? (If so, explain.)

Chapter 12

Tough Choices to Make

Given the cultural society we have today, I could easily have given up this struggle, letting Cal just do his own thing and me mine. But I knew that was not God's choice for us.

To be a proper partner to Cal, when our communication and understanding had broken down, the Lord called me to make a serious choice. The year of our twenty-fifth wedding anniversary Cal was feeling so low, so neglected that he thought our marriage was over. Don't let anyone tell you otherwise … Male Menopause and Midlife Crisis are real! And it can be the absolute P-I-T-S!

My home-based business, back then, was going well. I had just reached the point where I was covering my monthly expenses (gas, spending money, etc.) and beginning to make a profit. I had even started making enough to purchase extras around the house. I was so PROUD to be earning money myself and wasn't draining the family budget for my selfish wants and desires. But then, Cal lost his job and things had to change.

Cal's long period of unemployment with months of disappointments didn't work well with the home-based public relations business I was building. Yet, on the practical side, it was difficult to see that giving up my revenue would be a good thing. Besides, I was excited that our children needed less of my time. I had looked forward to *my time.*

Because Cal, the financially responsible partner, wasn't employed, he resented my efforts to work, which made no sense. We needed someone to contribute to our family finances.

He started pointing out how other couples we knew were divorcing. He'd say, "See, it's because she's started working outside their home." I would disagree, saying, "But that makes no sense for us! I have always had a job. Honestly, someone needs to pay the bills! I know you are hurting and frustrated at the lack of response to resumes being sent out, but this is hard for me too."

We began planning a new seminar business idea Cal had come up with. There were too many complications, however, around Cal's male ego and my being his wife for us to work well together. The worst thing was our different work styles. I plan ahead and eliminate every negative possible while Cal did things on the fly at the spur of the moment and viewed every negative that I brought up as depressing criticism.

The seminar business never took off and he resented my home-based PR company so much that one day I came home from an appointment to find his wedding ring on the chair in my office with a note saying I should close my business or the marriage was over. He failed to respond to my phone calls and took all day to come home. We finally had an in-depth discussion, which we should have had a long time before.

During these emotional discussions, he continued to ask me to give up my PR business and help him find a job. I felt confused. My business was paying some of the bills. How could I make this decision?

I went to my closest Christian friends, seeking prayer and guidance. They told me to do what was right for me, but something didn't feel right with giving up and just doing my own thing. The Holy Spirit contradicted their advice.

I turned to my trusted prayer partner, Jackie, who suggested I might be emasculating Cal through my business. Then, the Lord began speaking to my heart saying, "What is best for you is what was best for *both* of you!"

This thought echoed what Gary Thomas says in *Sacred Influence*: "What's good for your husband is good for the two of you. A healthy husband is a happier husband, a more caring husband, and a more attentive husband."[1]

The Lord reminded me of Proverbs 19:21 which says, "Many are the plans in a person's heart, but it is the Lord's purpose that prevails."

This very issue had almost destroyed our marriage. If I thought that my period of "fulfilling" my self had been destructive, I had no idea!

Even though I slowed down my PR business involvement, I suffered attacks in doing even small projects for existing clients. My largest client couldn't pay me and I stopped providing them credit. I realized God was again calling for my *complete* commitment to him. He was saying, "Surrender it all." He wanted to be the Lord of my life—again!

Cal was always respectful of me, encouraging me to do those things that helped me grow and be fulfilled. But even after I had given up my own business, in his own pain, I felt like he was attempting to limit me, to hold me back, perhaps unconsciously, wanting to bring me down to his place of misery.

As I refused to be dragged down, I made him feel I was not the supportive wife he married. Though I had rough moments, my faith encouraged my creative, positive, can-do attitude.

This got me through, but often made Cal, who was still an unbeliever, feel even more alone. At the time, I could only pray that this would eventually turn his heart toward God.

Cal was forced, by his periods of unemployment, to be a stay-at-home husband and he hated it. He wasn't supposed to be there! Watching me do work in my home-based business didn't help.

I had been able to deal with restlessness by immersing myself in business or writing. It helped me, but poor Cal kept looking for something to do and didn't have the confidence to try something entrepreneurial of his own. This was perhaps due to his strong need for security, which he adopted from his parents' financial struggles.

During our biggest, most serious argument time, it felt like my best friend disappeared whenever Cal's jobs went away. The differences that made us a good couple drove us apart. We decided to write letters to each other expressing the hurts we were each feeling.

His letter expressed his need for me to be there and help rescue him. He felt pressure from my working. I had humiliated him in public. I had undermined his disciplining of the kids. I was tired whenever he wanted to go out at night. I had a lack of sensitivity over his medical concerns. I was sharing too much of our personal life with others (through prayer requests). He thought I wasn't being realistic about how serious our financial situation was. I yelled in front of the kids. He reminded me that during our dating period, I often backed down whenever I disagreed with something but that now I tended to argue more.

I responded by apologizing for being so argumentative, but I also reminded him that he had actually suggested I start the PR company. Now, I felt confused that he wanted me to close the company. I reminded him that as my hard work was finally paying off, my income would help us pay our bills until he obtained another job. I admitted that having a successful business helped me cope with my not being good enough issues from childhood, especially with my difficult past career history.

I wrote, "I want very badly to maintain a satisfying balance between helping the family financially and being your wife. I know in my heart that the real problem here is that you don't have a meaningful, exciting productive career direction.

"I love you more than you will ever know. That's why this hurts so much, but I don't think you really understand or trust me right now because of your own pain. Tell me what you really need from me … specifics, please. How can I help you?"

His responding letter said, "What you don't seem to understand is that you are going on doing your own things and you ignore me. I feel neglected, unappreciated, and taken for granted. I feel disrespected when we are out in public. You are so independent that you don't seem to need me. You have taken the kids away from my Jewish faith and I hate that you always try to control me.

"I will love you always, but this is difficult for me. You must change or it will affect our relationship. I want our marriage to be a partnership."

We struggled for several days to understand each other's hurt.

Cal was falling apart and blaming me for his misery in the marriage. I knew that since he was struggling to find his own career direction, it was difficult for him to watch me grow in my own home-based business venture.

It was obvious I had to learn ways to become *his* best friend again. Things like not fighting over the unimportant stuff, working on not being so selfish, having more excitement before going on a trip, and being more spontaneous (and joyful) about planning BBQs and picnics. He shared that he felt taken for granted and unappreciated.

In *Sacred Influence*, I found what could be the reason. In pure laziness of being married about twenty-five years, I had failed to recognize or show appreciation for Cal's strong points.[2]

Cal's letter to me also addressed my independence and control issues. He wanted our relationship to be more of a partnership. He needed me to be more hospitable with his family. He requested I not ask for advice unless I planned to use it or, at least, give it some consideration. He wanted us to watch each other's TV shows more.

He also pointed out my good points. He acknowledged I tried to keep him healthy, that I didn't question his wisdom about family finances, that I didn't bug him about unemployment, that I was a sensitive mother to the kids, that I handled the busywork with the kids—homework, driving, scholarships, school meetings, etc., that I was excellent in helping our son find solutions for his learning disability, and that I gave him freedom to go out and do Karaoke with friends.

In my letter, I also pointed out Cal's good points—that he was a responsible, good, caring, involved father. He was fun to be with. He was the life of the party. He endeavored to be a good provider in good and bad times. He was good with car repairs and computers. He kept mechanical things going. He had been supportive of my return to school, my volunteer work, my return to work full-time, and my starting a business. He had his mother's tender heart. He was my protector and always came to my rescue.

I began to realize how hard it was for him to see me pursuing my dreams when he was having his own career struggles.

Pushing away the anger I sometimes felt, I spent an entire year searching Scripture for answers.

> "The wise woman builds her house, but with her own hands the foolish one tears hers down." (Proverbs 14:1)

I'd been through Proverbs twice before. But apparently, I hadn't been able to see this message.

An encouraging difference in the balance between my career and Cal's pain began to occur as I took a part-time position as office manager at my church. It kept me "in my place," gave me an opportunity to make my own decisions and helped with family finances. It provided a good balance.

Cal and I usually communicated well. Our written responses helped us both acknowledge each other's needs and move toward making necessary changes that saved our marriage.

I was constantly being brought back to the unconditional surrender stage—no matter what stage my life was in at the moment!

Chapter Wrap-Up:

How have you had to adjust to support your spouse? Have they adjusted to support you?

What decisions have you had to make that you didn't want to in order to help your marriage grow?

Write a letter to your husband today telling him all the things you appreciate about his role in your life.

Chapter 13

Crossroads of Marriage

I took a moment to explore why and how I decided to get married. The back cover of *Creative Counterpart* states, "A Creative Counterpart is more than just a helper. She is a woman who, having chosen the vocation of wife and mother, decides to learn and grow in all the areas of this role."[1]

As I think back, I'm not sure I really ever *chose* to be a wife and mother. Oh, yes, I agreed to marry Cal and bear his children, but when I graduated from high school in the late 1960s, girls were at a crossroads.

Many got married because it was the thing every young woman did at the time. Some continued on to college. Yet, college back then was often used as the place to find a good man to marry so he could take care of you. A few who went on to college did so for professional career reasons, but they were still viewed as mavericks back in the day. Of course, there were the hippies and free love advocates too. Those lifestyles seemed to be our only choices and role models.

Since I had already found my man, college was, initially, more of an opportunity to get away from my parents so I could think things through. Though I knew Cal and I would marry someday, we both wanted to finish college and then get married.

Our choice to marry at age twenty, in a sense, was forced by my parents' attempts to keep us apart. Let me be clear. I don't regret that decision at all. I always loved Cal and we had a great marriage, but I just question whether or not mine was really an *informed choice*.

Given my relatively young age, I probably didn't explore all the options or, more correctly, understand I had options. I'm not sure, but I think a lot of my disillusionment as a wife and mother may have revolved around this fact.

Was I a product of my circumstances or had I truly made an informed choice that would have allowed me to "decide to learn and grow in all areas of this role"? I think today's young women do have the ability to make a clearer choice than I was given. Options are much more varied now.

However, choice or not, given my personality and workaholic tendencies, I might have found myself a lonely career woman without husband, children, or grandchildren if I'd gone another way. For that reason, alone, I'm glad there were fewer options for me.

An article in the Los Angeles Times entitled, "A Dream Denied: They Wanted It All" states, "Now some women are finding they've lost something precious—motherhood." Author Lynn Smith illustrated what my own life was geared toward for a while, "We were adamant about redressing the lives of our mothers, the desire to be somebody, to have work that mattered, to have our own money."[2]

But Ecclesiastes 1:17 says that the "understanding of wisdom … is a chasing after the wind."

Even as I attempted to tell our story, all my searching is really only for me and may well be a chasing after the wind for others. As I learned an understanding of wisdom, our marriage indeed survived and began to thrive. When taken in biblical context, Solomon was the wealthiest man on earth in his time—perhaps why he found things meaningless. My life and struggles have not been meaningless. Tough at times, but never meaningless. My wisdom gained was very specifically related to my personal relationships and through life I have discovered relationships to be far more important than things will ever be.

Once again I found help in Gary Thomas's *Sacred Influence*. "Marriage is about choosing to allow the strong points of your marriage to be the dominant points, the area you *choose* to focus on. Where you absolutely can't meet, you find a way to detour … Instead of obsessing over your differences, think about the one or two things that you truly enjoy doing together."[3]

How true that advice was for us. Cal and I moved through this life as a team. I believe true soul mates are those who successfully accept the opposing traits of their partner and utilize their differences to create a stronger partnership. They take what is missing in one to strengthen the other. As we approached our fiftieth wedding anniversary, we celebrated our differences. We remained partners in life, working as a team to become what God wanted us to be—together.

Earlier, during my workaholic, self-denial process, I came across this Scripture.

> "But seek first his kingdom and his righteousness, and all these things will be given to you as well." (Matthew 6:33)

I learned to focus on God first, not my career or even my family. Through this difficult process, I initiated a new lifestyle and was beginning to truly give my life over to the Lord. I began starting my days with prayer, reading Scripture and a devotional to hit my reset button and reset for my new day. I would journal the answers the Holy Spirit led me to.

And I continued to open potential employment doors, but I calmed myself down to a more manageable pace. I prayed over opportunities before responding. I asked the Lord to open and close doors as he wanted. As I continued with my morning Bible study and sought the Lord's counsel, I knew God would direct my career path if I would let him and if I would follow the wisdom of his Word.

> Whatever you do, work at it with all your heart, as working for the Lord, not for human masters, since you know that you will receive an inheritance from the Lord as a reward. It is the Lord Christ you are serving. (Colossians 3:23–24)

Allen Jackson, author of *Intentional Faith Aligning Your Life with the Heart of God*, states, "Working as if it's a form of worship can change the way you think about your occupation. *Work* is not a new four-letter word. It's an opportunity to worship and to share the good news of God with the world around us."[4]

My own workaholic drive has represented the wrong focus. It encouraged my prideful self. During my employment waiting periods, I vowed to keep jobs in their rightful place.

Jackson believes millennials (with very different work ethics from prior generations) "reflect a tremendous opportunity ... They prefer work that satisfies rather than work that simply pays well. They want to experience life, express creativity and experience personal growth. All of which, if properly directed, can be expressions of a meaningful faith, particularly when expressed in the workplace."[5]

I could learn a few things from these young people. Even today, there seems to be so much God still needs to change in me. I just pray I will continue to be open to his molding of my character.

God continued to open my eyes to the insidious pride problems in my life that were blocking me from just being a *believer in Christ* to becoming a *Christ-follower*. Christ-followers replace pride with humility because they know who they are in Christ.

But pride kept rearing its ugly head in more ways than one. I would ask for God's help, but I didn't have the patience to wait for his answer. I have a very creative mind, which causes me to flit from one idea to another. I would immediately jump into the planning stages without even a second thought of involving the Lord. I trusted myself and plunged forward. This usually caused doors to immediately close much to my frustration. Then I would cover up and make excuses for the failure. While I overcame in one area, a new one always seemed to arise. Whenever I fail to trust the Lord, I find myself dealing with pride. It's human pride that makes me think I know better than God does. But I was warned...

> "Do not conform to the pattern of this world, but be transformed by the renewing of your mind." (Romans 12:2)

If I could renew my mind, I could change my attitude. Humility wasn't about seeing myself as a lower status or thinking less of myself. It's simply thinking of myself less. True humility is using good, sober judgment and not making myself more important by my own accomplishments. I heard a pastor once state in a sermon, "Emphasizing our own importance causes us to become an important human 'doing' instead of an important human 'being' and creates a harried lifestyle of trying to keep up with our own self-imposed activities rather than being quiet and waiting on God."

The Lord just wants us to be. He wants us to be empty vessels ready to be filled.

> "Those who cleanse themselves ... will be instruments for special purposes, made holy, useful to the Master and prepared to do any good work." (2 Timothy 2:21)

We can misuse our gifts if we use them only to benefit ourself. Gifts can also be rendered ineffective, if we are hurt or damaged through life (as I had been).

Jesus Christ is our healing. He is my way back to wholeness. (Romans 8:18–24) explains our need for the inevitable suffering we experience and the eventual hope provided by the Holy Spirit in our lives. Only God's Spirit knows the heart and mind of God—we surely don't! So often I've tried to fix things for others, rather than just listening and being led by the Holy Spirit to action. I need to understand the Word and be more prayerful before venturing out on anything. I have learned to be still and am getting better on waiting on the Lord.

Chapter Wrap-Up:

Did you always want to be married and have kids or did it just happen to you?

How are you and your spouse facing life as a team?

What do you enjoy doing together?

When you stop to be quiet, what things do you think about?

This week, take time to simply sit and listen to God. Don't speak, just be still and listen.

Chapter 14

How the Scriptures Continued to Guide Me

I cooperated with the Lord to preserve and enhance my marriage to Cal as I searched through Scripture during the worst times of struggle.

First, I found Scripture warning against false gods.

> "Do not bow down before their gods or worship them or follow their practices. You must demolish them and break their sacred stones to pieces. Worship the Lord your God, and his blessing will be on your food and water. I will take away sickness from among you…" (Exodus 23:24–25)

Then I read Scripture about the city of Tyre—a popular locale for business in ancient times. Ezekiel 27 highlights all the many nations that did business with Tyre, but the prophets warned that this great city would be destroyed because God was not part of their successful works. I took this as another direct warning to be careful about my love for business.

Then, although Proverbs 7:6–11 and Proverbs 7:21–27 speak of a prostitute seducing a young man, the verses spoke clearly to me as a warning not to be seduced away from my marriage by the false gods of selfishness, pride, or my career.

As I continued to study my Bible, it became evident God was the way through the quagmire of my life and career. My new direction was becoming clear and it wasn't a question of making money.

> "Choose my instruction instead of silver, knowledge rather than choice gold, for wisdom is more precious than rubies, and nothing you desire can compare with her." (Proverbs 8:10–11)

Mark 2:21–22 warned me about placing new wine in old wine skins. I'd heard it before, but then I finally understood it's meaning for my own life. I could not combine this new faith with my old way of thinking—my life would simply fall apart. I needed to make a *complete* change.

Mark 3:25 warned me about a house divided—it won't stand. How much clearer could God get?

I had been unfaithful to Cal with my business and we appeared to have been going separate ways because I was off doing my business and unemployed Cal was left at home in hurt and pain. Our house was divided!

Armed with these Scriptures under my belt, I prayed to follow the Lord wholeheartedly. I was led to pray for Cal too—for more workers in the field to speak to him (Matthew 9:37–38). I prayed to be able to obtain Christian speaking engagements, making money little by little, but still seeking to trust and fear the Lord for my future.

HOW THE SCRIPTURES CONTINUED TO GUIDE ME   123

I wanted to serve him in faithfulness. I wanted to throw away the gods worshiped by my forefathers, like workaholism.

Once again familiar Scripture reminded me that I was to be a wise woman building my house, not destroying it (Proverbs 14:1).

Even though I felt I was going in the direction God was showing me, the Lord kept providing warnings from his Word.

I was reminded of how Delilah's deceptive behaviors toward Samson highlighted the emasculation that made him feel like less of a man—something I felt I had been doing to Cal (Judges 16:6–21).

While we struggled through our relationship and financial problems, Cal's dad, Barney, died. Scripture reminded me to be very sensitive to my husband and not to be a quarrelsome wife, especially when he was experiencing such pain (Proverbs 19:13).

Years later, as I read *Sacred Influence*, the author's suggested questions for anyone dealing with what I had experienced seemed appropriate. "Can you maintain a soft heart over past hurts, patiently praying for long-term change? Or will you freeze him in his incapacities with judgment, resentment, condemnation, and criticism? Can you maintain a *nurturing* attitude instead of a judgmental one?"[1]

Themes of obedience and submission continued to surface through Scripture. As much as I longed to do Christian speaking, it was not the right time. I struggled to keep my eyes on the Lord and be released from the snare. I diligently studied Scripture, seeking the Lord and his promise that I would lack no good thing.

During this process I learned more about Cal serving as my head. I learned I must allow him to be the covering for my head and that I was Cal's glory. I learned I was created for Cal and he was created for me. Cal was my sign of authority (1 Corinthians 11:3–12).

This reference to Cal being my head, my covering, and my sign of authority can be confusing. It has its roots in the Middle East, but means that God has given men the responsibility to care for and protect their wives and families. Conversely, I was intended to be Cal's glory as described in Proverbs 31:11. This woman's "husband has full confidence in her." In other words, a godly woman makes her husband look good.

As mentioned before, if the kids wanted to go to a church event, the Lord had me tell them to go ask for their dad's permission. By doing so, I was respecting Cal as the final decision maker. This worked out well, but he would sometimes get upset about what the kids were being taught at church. Yet he'd made the decision to allow them to go, so it wasn't my fault. I couldn't be blamed. Clearly God's system was best.

I received specific husband and wife instructions from Ephesians 5 about submitting to one another out of reverence for Christ and how wives and husbands should treat their spouse.

And I finally began to understand headship. "The husband is the head of the wife as Christ is the head of the church, his body, of which he is the Savior" (Ephesians 5:23). Even though Cal did not know Christ, I did and felt called to give Cal his rightful place.

The Word reminded me of the importance of yielding to God's overall plan. In my case yielding to Cal was the key. In addition, I chose to treat him as if he were already a believer. I think that move on my part helped to lead Cal in his search for Messiah Jesus. It became an example to him for how a godly marriage should be.

But I wish to caution all women in this regard.

The Bible does *not* teach the subjugation of women to men and submission does not mean "inferior." God cherishes men and women equally. As Gary Thomas says in *Sacred Influence*, "Helping may be a defining role to which God calls married women, but it's not the defining role." Finally, the context of submission is *mutual*.[2]

If a man is disrespectful or condescending toward his wife and tries to justify this behavior by his position as the head of the household, this is clearly not marriage as God intended, and it is not what is taught in Scripture concerning the roles of husband and wife.[3]

So please know that if you're in that kind of unbalanced relationship, God is *not* telling you simply to submit. He wants you to create a balanced and equal relationship based on God's love for both you and your partner.

As time went by, I learned to delight in the things of the Lord and, over time, he has given me much more than the desires of my heart (Psalm 37:4).

Through the study of my Bible, I learned that pride in my own business was an addiction just like alcohol or drugs. I got high on the pride and my accomplishments found in business ownership. Had my business been successful at the expense of our family, it would certainly have been like the fading flower demonstrated in Isaiah 28:1.

I also recognized I had to stop trusting in man's ways of success (Isaiah 2:22).

But as I was finding encouragement in Scriptures and feeling like God was there for me, Cal became more and more depressed. Some days he just seemed to shut down. He kept saying he felt forgotten by me. Then the next day he would say Jesus was in his heart. I was on a rollercoaster of *his* making.

Again, Thomas's words from *Sacred Influence* spoke to me. "In the midst of living with this kind of frustration, it can be easy to forget the things that first drew you to your man: his sense of humor, his thoughtfulness, his spiritual depth, or any number of other strengths."[4] With Cal and me it was also his commitment to family.

But the Lord promised me through more Scriptures that he would not reject descendants of Israel and he wouldn't reject me, even with all that I had done wrong! God's promises are so good. I prayed that Cal would hear God wherever he went and be inspired to fear God.

But from what Cal was sharing, it seemed like God was being hidden from him.

As I changed my life, these verses from 2 Timothy became a promise, but only if I followed God obediently.

> "Flee the evil desires of youth, and pursue righteousness, faith, love and peace, along with those who call on the Lord out of a pure heart. Don't have anything to do with foolish and stupid arguments, because you know they produce quarrels. ... Yet the Lord rescued me from all of them. In fact, everyone who wants to live a godly life in Christ Jesus

will be persecuted, while evildoers and impostors will go from bad to worse, deceiving and being deceived. But as for you, continue in what you have learned and have become convinced of, because you know those from whom you learned it, and how from infancy you have known the holy Scriptures, which are able to make you wise for salvation through faith in Christ Jesus. All Scripture is God-breathed and is useful for teaching, rebuking, correcting, and training in righteousness, so that the servant of God may be thoroughly equipped for every good work." (2 Timothy 2:22–23, 3:11–17)

Scripture was allowing me to flee my evil desires and avoid arguments as I changed my life. And the Lord stood by my side and gave me strength (2 Timothy 4:17).

As hard as all of this seemed, God encouraged me along the way with even more Scripture.

> "Ask *and* keep on asking and it will be given to you; seek *and* keep on seeking and you will find; knock *and* keep on knocking and the door will be opened to you. For everyone who keeps on asking receives, and he who keeps on seeking finds, and to him who keeps on knocking, it will be opened." (Matthew 7:7–8 AMP)

But I always had much work to do.

The Word continued to speak to me of humbling those who walk in pride (Daniel 4:37). And I was instructed to use the gifts I'd received to serve others (1 Peter 4:10).

Toward the end of that uncertain year of financial struggles, I reflected back and realized our children were not destitute. Praise God, the enemy had not prevailed. Cal was less angry and depressed. God had kept his promises!

What a beautiful promise for my own life I found that year. We would triumph and God would rebuild. We would never be uprooted. Just as he said in the book of Amos, God rebuilt everything so wonderfully (Amos 9:13–15)!

Chapter Wrap-Up:

What Scriptures help you feel stronger in the Lord? Write them out.

What Scriptures seem too hard for you to understand or are intimidating? Write those out too and consult a commentary or pastor for help.

Chapter 15

Hit From All Sides!

My parents were amazing people. Dad had graduated from high school at age sixteen to become an international attorney following three and a half years as a Japanese POW during World War II. Mom was an accomplished woman who got a Master's degree at a time when most women didn't even go to college. She actually saved the lives of WWII fighter pilots with a design change she made while working at an aircraft company.

At the end of their respective careers, they retired to a peaceful farm in upstate New York. My brother, Dave, graduated from college and moved to the farm, where he started a solar energy business. Our little brother, Jon, brain damaged as a toddler by his DPT shot, was moved to a group home nearby.

Life was good for all of us.

As our parents aged, Julie and I began making annual trips back to see them.

When our eighty-seven-year-old mother fell and broke her hip two days before one of our visits, we spent much of that visit cooking meals and cleaning for Dad and Dave. Our vacation included daily visits to Mom in the hospital where she was in good spirits and healing well. Knowing Mom would need help with housework, I arranged for a local caregiving company to provide light housekeeping services and for Meals on Wheels deliveries before we left.

I felt blessed that we could do these tasks for them and that our family was still intact.

Two years later our entire California family visited my parents and stayed in a beautiful bed and breakfast where we held joint eighty-ninth and ninetieth birthday celebrations for them.

We had no idea how much of a blessing the memories would become when just eight months later we would lose Mom to a stroke.

Her death began a devastating chain of events for all of us.

Following our mother's sudden death, Dad stressed over financial worries coupled with guilt for not completing her will before she died. All of this heaped on top of lingering thoughts of unpaid taxes and his refusal to hire an accountant to help. He refused to have the family attorney help settle the estate. He was a proud and stubborn (though loving and generous) man who felt embarrassed by his predicament. I think this additional stress contributed to the escalation of his developing dementia, which none of us recognized at the time.

He began to make rash and unwise financial decisions when it was clear he had nothing to worry about. Nonetheless, he felt stressed because Mom had always paid the bills and kept their finances straight. Following Mom's death, he felt helpless and lost, not only emotionally but also financially.

During our second visit that year, Julie slowly obtained Dad's permission to organize and file his papers and a trusting relationship developed between them. This often happens between grandparents and grandchildren. I think Dad still saw me as the rebellious sixteen-year-old I'd been forty-five years before! It is often difficult for senior parents to see their offspring as the professionals they have become. As parents age, a role reversal begins taking place.

Dad was very protective of his filing system, which was scattered all over the floor and couches on one side of the living room. Most of the time he remained secretive and protective of his finances, making it very difficult for us to really help.

As our visits became more frequent, we began sorting through legal issues and the back taxes, all complicated further by Dad's extreme privacy and complete lack of a filing system.

Realizing that Dad no longer had good judgment on legal issues was particularly difficult.

I don't think either my brother nor I caught his decline fast enough because of what I call his "Intelligent Dementia."

For example, when he had a Mini-Mental State Exam, he was asked what day it was to which he responded that if they would give him the newspaper, he would tell them.

He remained lucid most of the time, though he seemed to become more and more stubborn. Things were very difficult to figure out and Mom was no longer there to ask.

Dad hadn't told us where all his other investments were. There was much we didn't know. And he was *extremely* adamant that *no one* was to have a Power of Attorney. He was going to handle everything himself!

It would have been so much easier had Mom and Dad discussed the future with us and faced the fact that one day they might not be able to handle legal or financial responsibilities. I could have been appointed guardian for Jon much earlier and one of us might have been designated as the Power of Attorney for both of our parents.

Since Dave, who never married, lived at the farm with Dad, he took over the difficult task of Dad's caregiving.

The message here is how important, though difficult, family discussions about end-of-life decisions are.

After experiencing this time in my life, my advice is to make sure everything is legally in place, just in case. Openly discuss the transfer of responsibilities from spouse down to a child, a trusted friend, or a fiduciary, making sure the chosen individuals are comfortable with their proposed roles. Discuss health care decisions and who would be best to help carry those desires out.

Following one of our trips, Julie and I had just returned to California, when Dave emailed.

"On Dad's way to church today he had a collision with a cow that was in the road. He says the cow ran into him, spun him around and the car went down a bank into the field—about 50 feet. He was unhurt, but the car has major damage. We don't know about the cow. It ran off."

Once Dad's car was repaired, he insisted upon driving himself to the attorney's office fifty miles away in wintry weather.

Then Dave discovered that Dad's medication was making him sleepy, causing additional driving concerns.

Dad was then diagnosed with cataracts, which leads to a decrease in vision. He was told by his doctor not to drive at night until after his cataracts surgery.

Dave shared that our normally law-abiding father had been stopped by the police twice because of his erratic nighttime driving. The police had called Dave to come get Dad several times!

Armed with this new information, Dave took the keys away from Dad. Dad was very upset.

Finally, Dave gave him an ultimatum. If the police called him to rescue Dad again, he would request that they suspend his license.

On top of this, Dad received his first speeding ticket ever!

Dave reached out to me for help, so I emailed the NY State DMV asking if there were a way to *anonymously* report an elderly parent as an unsafe driver.

They explained that Dad needed another Driver Review. They wouldn't just take away his license. Since he had gone through this once before, he probably wouldn't suspect that we had filed the form. We hoped this would help him to listen to Dave about his driving.

Dave sent me an update:

"He's really very depressed about the possibility of losing his license. I talked with him this AM about the caregiving company having a driving service. He was very enthusiastic about it. He is willing to use it."

Dad remained hopeful that he would get his license back, though none of us wanted him driving and we all knew he shouldn't.

With the help of the local attorney friend of Dad's, we were finally able to settle Mom's estate three years after her death.

Shortly after settling the estate, Dad's confusion, which had improved greatly, took a turn for the worse. It was almost as if he had held himself together to get things done and then just fell apart.

Emails from Dave began describing episodes of confusion and disturbing behavior.

During our next visit we noticed Dad had become more compliant, but still refused to use a walker, wheelchair, or the motor cart in Walmart. He was often fixated on issues like thinking the attorneys had forgotten to include my mother's cousins whom she had outlived! He thought they should have been included in the settlement, but her cousins were long gone. People with dementia often fixate on unrealistic or nonsensical issues.

My own stress over Cal's health issues caused me to confuse things too during this time. I've never been good with names, but now I had trouble being able to access the right word for things. Then my communication with Julie became strained due to all the stress. She thought I was bringing drama to the situation, but I'm not the drama-type!

Prior to leaving for California, I set things in motion for Dad to have a caregiver.

But just before our next visit, Dave was at his wits end and desperate when he emailed:

"Dad needs to be in a nursing home or assisted living center. Our top priority when you are here will be to find an appropriate place. I can't deal with him anymore! How do we get him in one? I haven't a clue how to start."

I had no idea of what to expect on our next visit and upon our arrival I found that, indeed, Dad looked and smelled like a homeless guy. How sad for an honored POW and someone so accomplished in his professional days.

So, Julie and I set to work. We took him to the local clothing store and got him suitable new clothes. We increased his caregiver hours and added personal care (help with bathing, dressing, grooming, etc.).

This certainly wasn't easy! He objected to spending money on these things, even if we told him we were buying them for him. He called it a waste of money. He couldn't understand the need for additional caregiving hours.

Over subsequent months, he finally adjusted to the idea of additional care and actually began to enjoy the extra attention he was receiving.

As I began to read the disturbing emails sent by Dave, I also knew we needed to find someone local to help coordinate the details of Dad's care. He'd been very secretive over his doctor visits, so I needed access to Dad's medical records.

Though Dave had done an admirable job in a difficult situation, he needed someone else to manage Dad's care so he could concentrate on his business. We found a Geriatric Care Manager in New York to coordinate Dad's care details. She was a member of the National Association of Professional Geriatric Care Managers.[1]

The Care Manager worked directly with Dad's caregiving company to provide needed services and she accompanied Dad to visits with new doctors. She coordinated with the home care company to have someone accompany him on follow-up doctor visits.

We no longer had to worry about Dad's safety, personal care, healthcare, and all that comes with a dementia diagnosis.

I encourage families to research this wonderful solution. The field of Geriatric Care Management helps all family caregivers, whether they live in the same town or thousands of miles away.

On our next visit, I was looking forward to an opportunity to relax and just be Dad's daughter for the first time in years.

It was not to be.

Both Julie and I saw more cognitive decline. His stubborn personality coupled with increasing dementia made him unsafe alone. He fell several times, scaring us. We faced the reality that 24/7 professional caregiving was becoming necessary.

Unfortunately, the agency and the remote location made it impossible to find continuous weekend and overnight care. This was par-

---

1   www.caremanagers.com

ticularly disturbing because Dave often left early and returned late on Saturdays. He had no weekend office staff to keep an eye on Dad.

The day I was returning to California and Dave was headed out for site surveys no one would be there for Dad.

With my past experience in an Assisted Living Community, I knew there was a possibility that I could find local Respite Care.[2]

I found an Assisted Living Community with a memory care unit nearby and they offered Respite Care.

We explained to Dad that since I was going home and Dave was leaving on business, we had found a really nice place for him to stay over the weekend.

Dad was very unsure when I dropped him off on Friday, but I assured him Dave would pick him up on Sunday. Dave said Dad seemed to enjoy his stay, though he kept talking about how much money it was costing. Dave tried to explain, but Dad didn't get the idea that it was much less than having home caregivers 24/7.

Dad shared that he had met an old friend and they had discussed their joint memory losses. The fact that Dad opened up and told Dave was such a breakthrough!

We had successfully allowed Dad to age in place using the homecare company for an additional year beyond what Dave had thought he could possibly handle.

---

[2] Assisted living communities sometimes offer this for families that need temporary care for aging loved ones. It is a nice way to check them out before a permanent move is made.

So, given Dad's recent history of falls, cognitive deficit, and his need for 24-hour care, we decided it was time for a permanent move to the Assisted Living Community. This provided us peace of mind, so we began preparing him for the move.

Dave shared, "Dad may have difficulty expressing himself and he's making up words to substitute for the ones he has lost. But he is still Dad inside there. He is still a lawyer, so we need to communicate to him in our words and actions that we are not opposing him."

This complicated the process for us because, though Dad was getting to like the community, he often talked about having been "hijacked."

It was heartbreaking to hear Dad say he felt like he'd been "hijacked." This was hard on all of us, but we knew it had to be done!

We did everything we could to make him feel at home there. We took his favorite French dressing, and pictures of his parents and other family pictures. We even made sure he had plenty of his junk mail to open, his favorite daily task.

Julie created a grandkid mail campaign, so he would get family mail at his new home.

We had so many things planned but barely two weeks into his move to the assisted living, he fell. At the hospital, they found he had pneumonia.

When he was first hospitalized, he just wanted out. But when I asked him on the phone how they were treating him, he responded, "Too well! They are spoiling me in this expensive hotel!"

He was still fixated on cost, even though we both told him that insurance was covering it.

I could hear his increasing confusion. I had serious concerns for both my dad and Cal's declining health. It was all happening at once. So difficult!

Finally (after almost a month), Dad was released from the rehab and back at the Assisted Living Community.

I had requested a conference call with his rehab team, which was wonderful! I was reassured he was making progress. I was able to ask important questions and found that his dementia was not as bad and he wasn't as confused as when either I spoke to him on the phone or when Dave visited him.

An assisted living representative visited Dad to be sure he still qualified to return to their community. We were excited to hear that Dad recognized her name on her nametag and that he was thrilled he would be returning to the Assisted Living Community soon.

When Dad was ready to leave, Dave and I decided it would be best for the Assisted Living Community to pick Dad up from the hospital to take him back to their community.

Since he would probably beg Dave to take him "home," we felt it would work out better in terms of his adjusting.

One blessing out of this bad situation for our Dad was that he got used to using the walker, which he had resisted before. He came back to the community using it.

The community was very attentive. They updated us both on Dad's progress and that he was settling in and enjoying the fellowship of other residents during bingo and other activities. We were very pleased with his care and happy that he was in a safe environment.

However, a short twenty-five days later, an email from Dave and the Assisted Living facility explained that one of their aides had noticed Dad had a cold and that there was blood in his urine. He had a catheter placed and intravenous antibiotics begun at the hospital. Following the treatment for the infection, they removed the catheter so he could return to assisted living. Once again, we were in a frustrating waiting game to see if Dad was okay without the catheter. Dad's hospital nurse explained that he couldn't return to the Assisted Living facility with a catheter.

In a phone call to Dad, I tried to encourage him to drink lots of liquids and be sure he got up to walk. When I explained that he was back in the hospital because of an infection, he stubbornly responded that he did *not* have an infection. He said that the blood in his urine was from grape juice he had spilled! This demonstrates how dementia can be. My dad was still smart, so he tried to figure out solutions. He obviously figured that if it's just grape juice, he should have been able to get out of the hospital. Intelligent Dementia again!

About four days into this hospital stay, I finally had a great phone call with my dad. With the infection gone, he was pretty alert. We talked about him going back to the Assisted Living Community in a day or two and that that was where he lived now. He said he would like to go home, but acknowledged he had no choice. This was good. He finally seemed resolved to the fact that he could not live at the farm again.

However, as it turned out, he was not able to function without the catheter, so we began making plans to move him to the VA Home Skilled Nursing Unit. The VA Home provided assisted living in a skilled nursing environment. This was what Dad needed at that point.

About a month into his move to the VA Home, Julie and I went for a visit to be sure he was properly settled in. He looked really good. He was mostly alert and they seemed to be treating him well.

They had great activities at the VA Home. The only thing we were disturbed about was that Dad seemed to have given up any attempts at rehab, so he spent his days in a wheelchair instead of using his walker. I wished I lived close enough to continue to encourage him to improve, but we were happy that Dad was safe and adjusting to his new home.

We were also very excited to learn that my brother's group home could bring Jon to visit Dad at the VA Home. They were able to see more of each other than before and this was good for both of them.

All and all, though this journey had been frustrating, difficult, and stressful, Dad was finally in a good place.

For over two years Dave had asked Dad to hire an accountant, but he constantly refused. He had always done his own taxes and he said he didn't want to burden an accountant with his piles of paper. We think he was probably more than a bit embarrassed too.

By this time, the IRS began sending threatening letters. This was particularly upsetting to Dave, because if Dad's property were seized it could have directly affected Dave's business. His shop was located on the farm.

The IRS would not accept Dave's limited Power of Attorney signature, so they refused the returns and the payments Dave had sent.

Dave showed Dad the IRS Power of Attorney form that he had to sign before any of us could even talk with the IRS on his behalf, but he flatly refused to sign it. He said he would hire the accountant himself, when he was ready.

During our next visit I took him to meet with the IRS, where they convinced him to sign the required IRS form to allow Dave's CPA to help untangle his tax mess.

Months later, his back taxes were finally prepared, ready to be signed, and a check was written to pay off all the back taxes and penalties.

However, we were back to square one, when Dad refused to sign the returns.

The CPA finally convinced him he knew what he was doing. He assured Dad that he had properly prepared the returns and that Dad should sign.

After eight long years, we were finally successful in handling the financial mess with the IRS. Dave successfully sent the IRS payment with Dad's signed IRS form and Dave never had to talk to Dad about his taxes again.

Chapter Wrap-Up:

Are you experiencing a time of difficulty? If so, these Scriptures for strength and answers might help.

"Consider it pure joy, my brothers and sisters, whenever you face trials of many kinds, because you know that the testing of your faith produces perseverance. Let perseverance finish its work so that you may be mature and complete, not lacking anything." (James 1:2–4)

"Blessed is the one who perseveres under trial because, having stood the test, that person will receive the crown of life that the Lord has promised to those who love him." (James 1:12)

"He gives strength to the weary and increases the power of the weak. (Isaiah 40:29)

Chapter 16

This Old Age Thing is Getting Serious for Us Too!

As we were struggling to properly care for my aging Dad with dementia, I found the following Scripture and admitted that someday it was going to apply to us too.

> "Very truly I tell you, when you were younger you dressed yourself and went where you wanted; but when you are old you will stretch out your hands, and someone else will dress you and lead you where you do not want to go." (John 21:18)

At this point in our story, I looked at some of the major changes that can take place with aging and relationships.

With age our muscles can lose flexibility and strength. This can affect balance, which can lead to falls in the elderly. Falls are of particular danger to seniors, as it proved to be for Cal.

Memory can decrease with age, too—it may take longer to learn new things or remember familiar words or names. Wow! I think that's happening to me too, but let's not talk about that!

As we aged as a couple, the things that drew me toward Cal in our early days changed. His health declined, altering physical abilities in many areas including physical intimacy.

His health problems led to his battle with depression and that changed him too, but he remained the same caring, sweet man somewhere way beneath on some days and close to the surface on others. He changed, but our commitment to one another didn't.

I found online that there could be medical reasons for the emotional changes I began seeing in Cal. It became obvious why he was sometimes a "grumpy old man." This helped me understand him better—at least in theory! Admittedly, sometimes the frustration got to me though.

"It is estimated that at least four to five million American men have low testosterone. If the doctor finds low testosterone along with other factors such as low sexual desire, erectile dysfunction, ejaculatory dysfunction, fatigue, muscle weakness, obesity, or an unstable mood, the doctor may prescribe testosterone replacement therapy," says Dr. Ridwan Shabsigh, head of the International Society of Men's Health and a urologist in New York City.[1]

That would certainly be enough to make me grumpy!

Another name for low testosterone is hypogonadism. "(Hypogonadism) in renal failure has a multifactorial etiology, including co-morbid conditions such as diabetes, hypertension, old age and obesity."[2]

Cal had both diabetes and kidney disease, so this made sense. Though not obese, he was getting older. We both were!

It was hard to maintain my own energy and drive when, for example, at Julie's birthday party, we were enjoying the young people's music and activities while my *old* spouse and another old man at the table were complaining about the music being too loud!

Certainly, there are reasons to become grumpy with old age and men are typically the first to get sick, but it didn't make things easy when I had such a "young-attitude" with so much energy and drive. But as things began to get serious for us, I unselfishly took charge.

Chapter Wrap-Up:

Do you need encouragement to cope with the challenges of family life? These Scriptures might help.

"Do not be anxious about anything, but in every situation, by prayer and petition, with thanksgiving, present your requests to God." (Philippians 4:6)

"Cast all your anxiety on him because he cares for you." (1 Peter 5:7)

"Jesus looked at them and said, 'With man this is impossible, but with God all things are possible.'" (Matthew 19:26)

Chapter 17

The Roller Coaster Ride of Declining Health

As I remembered the terrible time we went through with Cal's previous heart issues. I knew we had to stick together as a team through his latest one, too.

My dad died the same year that Cal had been having fainting spells, which he didn't want to worry me about. If I'd known I would have gotten him to the doctor sooner. Praise the Lord, God took care of him though! Due to the fainting spells, his driver's license had been taken away until we could rectify the issue.

His doctor determined a pacemaker/defibrillator would need to be implanted. After the surgery, he was sent home and I had to diligently take his vitals. All was good.

But the next morning he ate nothing for breakfast and took no insulin.

As I prepared to leave for work, I suddenly heard him snore the loudest snore I'd ever heard! It was a frighteningly horrible sound that I'd never heard before. It wasn't normal! Already on edge having to be his nurse, I ran in to see him with his eyes wide open but, praise the Lord, he was breathing and becoming alert again. I called 911.

His defibrillator had activated, which turned out to be a good thing, because obviously his heart had stopped and it got him going again. How incredibly scary!

His blood pressure was too low, so they rushed him back to the hospital where they kept him to adjust his medications and fluids.

It was always so hard for Cal to be in the hospital, but he was making the best of it.

We monitored his water retention and hoped his kidneys could get back to normal. (He had had some kidney damage over the years, so this was another concern we lived with.)

While I sat in Cal's hospital room, I would write in my journal.

> "The date on the board in Cal's hospital room is exactly 5 months since my dad died. I finally let some tears come … Not sure I have properly grieved Dad's death with everything else I have been facing."

Cal's Nephrologist (kidney doctor) had been concerned about Cal's kidney function. But, we got good news considering everything we'd just been through. The Nephrologist came in for the report on his kidneys. He was very positive and thought we could get Cal back to his normal kidney numbers, once his heart stabilized. The threat of dialysis was over. All appeared to be good.

But things can change in an instant.

Cal was released from the hospital after six days, but we were home only long enough for me to run to the pharmacy for some new meds, when I had to call 911 again. His BP was once again dangerously low.

ER doctors determined he had too much potassium in his body, though they had been loading him with it the day before.

Cal became nauseated with the potassium-removing treatments and his claustrophobia made the vaporizing mask over his face very scary.

The next day, he was moved to ICU and was actually feeling pretty good and he ate breakfast. But they kept monitoring him to determine what was going on.

The following day he continued to feel pretty good.

But then they found a blood clot in his left arm, which though it wasn't the dangerous kind, made him very concerned. His blood thinner was adjusted to make it pass.

We had another difficult night facing this new stress, but things were still moving forward.

Two days later, though it was a good day, was particularly hard for Cal as he continued to worry about the clot and remained in the hospital. They would not release him until he was sufficiently mobile and his potassium levels had been corrected.

Finally, they decided that his cardiologist would do the procedure *after* he went home and stabilized for a while. It appeared that we were on the upswing!

Cal was finally released seven days after this second ER visit.

I had always had to help him carefully monitor his food intake for the diabetes, but at this point the water retention and potassium levels became additional concerns. I had returned to work, so Julie checked on him and reported his breakfast details to me and left him with carefully measured ingredients for his turkey sandwich lunch.

It became critically important to measure quantities for any foods that might contain salt (sodium). Everything seems to be made with salt! Salt made him thirsty, which made him retain water and caused the need for him to take more diuretics, which could affect his kidneys negatively. One of the first things I had to change was buying low sodium turkey for his sandwiches.

Some nights we ended up with two different meals. I had to be sure I was getting enough potassium (important for those with healthy hearts), so I had to have some foods that he couldn't have. Wow, was that difficult!

Since, clearly, I had to make some major lifestyle changes, we held a meeting with our kids to decide what to do. I had to monitor everything Cal consumed, including all meals and snacks, though it drove him nuts having to write it all down and rehash every night what he'd eaten during the day. But it had to be done.

I began keeping a log of how much sodium was in his foods. We avoided processed foods, which contain a lot of salt and no more visits to his favorite fast-food restaurants. He couldn't have manufactured soups either.

His suggested intake was 2,000mg per day. For a person without health problems, a normal intake of sodium per day is 3,500mg—mostly from processed foods.

We had to learn what foods had potassium in them, too, so he would know what he couldn't eat. For instance, he could no longer have tomatoes or avocados. Praise God, things eventually got better as his heart strengthened and I found a delicious low sodium spaghetti sauce, which he could have occasionally. Though his potassium levels could be monitored through frequent blood tests, there was absolutely no way for him to tell in between blood tests where his potassium level was. This was stressful when he ate fast-food French fries too often. Fries have issues of potassium *and* sodium! What was I to do?

> *Note: The FDA doesn't regulate labels to indicate amounts of potassium in foods and whenever potassium is listed as an ingredient it is because, in healthy people, our bodies need a certain amount of potassium for our hearts. So, it is purely at the discretion of the manufacturers to list it as an ingredient.*

I learned tricks like how to remove potassium from potatoes, so for dinner I was able to prepare mashed potatoes or oven fries. I made him an adjusted main dish from a recipe where I could easily remove the salt. I "allowed" him to have a very small amount of margarine on his vegetables.

Then his nutritionist told us that white bread was better for him because whole wheat bread tends to have more potassium in it. What a job it was changing him from the foods that were once healthy for both of us to the foods that would keep him healthy and out of the hospital.

And of course, things like the whole wheat bread are important to keep *me* healthy! We were just so very different again. The very foods he couldn't have were critical to maintaining my own health.

"How long is this going to last?" I would ask the Lord.

Just out of curiosity, I took my blood pressure during this time of stress. It was normally low, but then it recorded as high normal! I knew it was the stress, but I also knew that somehow I needed to take care of myself through all of this.

Having worked with seniors, I knew the statistics about how the caregiving spouse frequently dies before the person they are caring for because they don't take care of themselves. I knew it would be important for me to take care of myself, so I could be there for him.

Finally, Cal stabilized and was committed to going to his many doctor appointments to keep him that way.

We tried to get out of the house, but by the time he got dressed, he'd decide he was just too tired to go out, so would take a nap instead.

But as we figured these things out, I had spent more and more time away from my job. I had to begin figuring out who could help Cal while I was out of the house. He wasn't ready to be on his own.

I prayed, evaluated, and pondered many nights over a class of wine and some mindless television. Was I better off working just part-time to get a later start in the morning, so I could be sure he ate a proper breakfast and then have our good friend come by in the afternoon until I got home from work? Or would Cal be okay in the morning until she came?

I just didn't know.

Knowing the importance of taking care of myself so I could be there for him, I decided to keep my full-time position for as long as possible. I loved my job and it was a good diversion for me. The idea was that it would take my mind off all Cal's health issues and alleviate some of our stressful financial concerns.

The plan worked and I returned to work full time. Gradually, I focused on the new responsibilities on my shoulders and our finances remained stable.

Each day Cal grew stronger and his head clearer. He gradually began to take care of himself and I was reassured by installing a Life Alert system for my own peace of mind.

Our friend served as his temporary caregiver for which we will be forever grateful. She was able to come most days just to check on him and report back to me through texts.

Eventually, we got good news that his potassium levels were fine, so that was one less issue to deal with—at least for a while! That said, he still had to be cautious in limiting his tomato and potato intake. He used white bread and hoped for the best before each blood test.

We tried to find a company that could address his dietary restrictions and deliver meals that were already prepared or easy for him to microwave. Unfortunately, that didn't work out financially and he had become such a picky eater that it was going to be up to me or nothing.

So, I spent weekends cooking his favorite meals, making adjustments on sodium and potassium levels, and freezing everything for him to use later.

Our friend did her best to keep him focused by asking what he had made for lunch and recording it for me. The frozen foods were nice for me, since all this stress was making me much more tired than usual. But we soon discovered he wasn't eating the prepared meals. He was back to eating his favorite fast-foods as soon as he got his licensed reinstated and he began taking small trips out of the house.

Changing our lifestyle was difficult, but coupled with his lack of discipline and his desire to just have whatever he felt like things remained stressful.

I did my best.

Every night when I got home I would look at the results in the food log I had designed. Some days he hadn't entered anything, so I had to ask him and log it for him.

I agonized about whether to reconsider quitting my job and work part-time or figure out something else. Cal didn't have an opinion because he said he was still dealing with his own "stuff." I just didn't know what to do! I valued his opinion and needed his support.

By Thanksgiving Day he had begun to retain so much liquid that he was miserable again. I could see the results of his stubborn eating behaviors in his bulging stomach. He was clearly consuming more salt than he should have been. The day after Thanksgiving, he asked me to take him to the hospital. He was so weak, water logged, and miserable that I took him to the hospital where his cardiologist could

THE ROLLER COASTER RIDE OF DECLINING HEALTH   157

complete the surgery to hook up the third lead of the pacemaker/defibrillator.

He spent the weekend at the hospital trying to lose water weight, so he would be ready for the surgery. He needed the cardiologist to hook up the third lead of the pacemaker/defibrillator to complete the initial surgery. Praise God, they found no evidence of the former blood clot in his arm, so the surgery was scheduled.

Following his surgery, Cal was told he needed to stay in the hospital for three more days to be sure everything was fine and to help him lose the rest of water he had been retaining.

He texted me while I was at work. "No...I'm not staying here for 3 more days!!!!!##" This is the way his text appeared on my phone. Honestly, I didn't need that reoccurring stress to hit me again as I was back at work dealing with hospice issues.

He stayed one more day, instead of three, and I picked him up after work. He began to settle in at home, once again.

His diet was pretty good because I only had things in the house that he could eat, but as he started getting out more he went back to his bad fast-food habits. Not only did he make wrong food choices for his diabetes, but also for his low sodium and potassium diet, when he ate out. I tried very hard not to be a nagging wife, but his poor decisions frustrated me. He didn't seem to care about his health and also became frustrated and depressed about it.

My stress level also changed during all of this. Not only was I dealing with Cal's health issues and special needs, but after we lost my dad I had to deal with Dad's disorganized finances and help Dave settle the estate.

During my stressful days, I constantly stopped and took deep breaths. I shut Cal off when he began stressing over something or other. I couldn't let his stress become my stress any more than it already had. I had to monitor my own BP to stay healthy for him.

Over time, I learned to let go of my worry about Cal. Though he was fully capable, he continued making wrong decisions that could potentially have dire consequences but I had to learn to let go and let God! Cal was an adult and he had to make his own choices.

Our relationship became strained and it was hard, but I continued to trust God to keep Cal motivated to do the right thing.

Cal's health was up to him. He knew what he needed to do and it was up to him to do it.

"The day a wife accepts the fact that she is not responsible for her husband's actions is one of the greatest days of her life … The wife is not responsible for the husband side of the marriage, *but* she *is* responsible for *all* of the *wife* side of marriage."[1]

As I backed off, Cal seemed to take better charge of his eating. I continued to bite my tongue and not nag.

At one point, I worried about him having dementia. I realized since Cal was no longer working, he got his days mixed up. Not because of dementia but simply because he didn't have to be any place at any particular time (except, of course, his doctor appointments).

I began thinking that perhaps Cal had to go through all these health struggles, disturbing times, and frustrations to make him turn more strongly to the Lord.

Duh, how could I be so stupid! As hard as it was, I had to be there for him but he had to find his own way. So hard, but so necessary.

I began to see myself as Cal's CEO (Chief Encouragement Officer) instead of an annoying nagger. But none of this was easy!

Chapter Wrap-Up:

What concerns do you have with the aging seniors in your life?

Are you or your spouse struggling with health issues that are affecting your family?

Are you the nagging wife described in Proverbs 21:19? If so, how is that working for you?

Chapter 18

Going in Different Directions: Cal's Last Few Months

Four years after I had lost my dad and Cal had his last successful heart surgery, Cal took a bad fall and I was diagnosed with breast cancer. It was another difficult time for both of us.

Cal didn't break anything in the fall, but he hurt his knee so badly he retreated to the couch for several months—a decision that affected his muscle strength.

Two weeks later I was facing a double mastectomy, but would be fine because they had caught my cancer early. Still, the stress of these health issues began to weigh on both of us. I felt anxious over everything in preparation for my surgery, so Cal reached out to his primary care doctor for help.

We felt we needed counseling to deal with the stress of the health issues and underlying anger we had both developed. Cal was willing to increase his depression meds, but needed support on how to care for himself during my forthcoming recovery from the surgery.

I had my own health questions. I was concerned over my quality of life through the recovery period. What would taking cancer meds do to my body? I praise the Lord I wasn't facing radiation or chemo, but I'd never had a major surgery. All I knew was that I had to do what I needed to do to live.

Ever the encourager despite his own health issues, Cal sent me this uplifting text in regard to my upcoming surgery: "Don't worry, you have always made the right decision!"

Something I really missed in our relationship during those years of aging was that I held back on sharing stressful things because of his heart condition. We had always been best friends and shared everything, but I felt I had to protect him. He still tried hard to be there for me, and we were still close like best friends, but it wasn't the same.

As the holidays approached, even though he didn't feel well from what we thought was just a bad cold, he had the windshield and mirror on my new car fixed and proudly reported to me that he had taken his morning pills and insulin shot. I always worried, if he forgot to take his meds.

But then, just before Christmas, Cal was sick all weekend with that bad cold and then I got a sore throat.

When the family left on Christmas Day, Cal said he needed to go to the doctor. I explained it would have to be the hospital since urgent care centers weren't open on Christmas Day. He hated hospitals, but that's where he wanted to go.

We spent the night in the ER and I stayed overnight with Cal. He had a very serious respiratory infection (RSV) and was placed into an isolation room. His issues with potassium surfaced again and more heart infarction (damage) was discovered. On top of that, he was retaining water.

Two days after Christmas he finally began doing better. He sounded better and the RSV seemed to be improving, so they sent him home.

But just when our hopes were once again buoyed, his potassium level dropped so low it caused his heart to stop and made the defibrillator go off and paramedics took him back to the hospital on New Year's Eve. I felt like we were going down the same path we'd been on four years before.

He spent New Year's Eve in the hospital, but I told him I couldn't stay with him overnight. I needed a solid night of sleep, especially if I were going to be back on this rollercoaster again.

Before I left for the night, I prayed that God would show me how to share Jesus in a meaningful way that would help Cal understand who he is and who we are in him. Cal thanked me for all I was doing and I responded with a variation of Philippians 4:13, "I can do all this through him who gives me strength."

I prayed Cal would only be sent home healthy and stable and that I would have the wisdom and strength to administer his pills and insulin until he could take over again. I prayed he would listen to me and would remain safe, motivated, and not depressed.

When Cal came home a week later, I prayed again for guidance and support. The first few days went well, but then, six days after his return home, Cal began to decline quickly. He could no longer stand on his own. I needed to finish final details in turning over my department to my boss before my surgery, which was scheduled for the end of that week and Cal couldn't be left on his own. I hired a caregiver to stay with him during the day.

Cal seemed to stabilize, but woke me up three times one night just to get him water.

Then Cal got up by himself, which freaked me out and I had trouble getting him back into his wheelchair.

One night, loving neighbors had to help me get him off the toilet.

My body developed a urinary tract infection (UTI) and a cold from the stress. I didn't feel like eating but forced myself to eat. I needed to keep my own strength up for my surgery.

A family conference was scheduled for the afternoon of January, 14, 2019 to discuss how we would handle Cal's increased needs. Since I needed sleep, we arranged for an overnight caregiver to come that night.

I'm so thankful that Julie gave her dad the option of staying at home with the caregiver or going back to the hospital to be checked out. He chose to stay home, so when his defibrillator went off that night, he was at home and had made the decision himself.

The Life Alert system called 911 for me, but the paramedics seemed to take forever. I begged Cal not to leave me, but this time it was all so different.

We still hadn't discussed having a Do Not Resuscitate (DNR) order so they tried bring to him back and took him to the hospital.

I will forever remember that night.

Suddenly, he was gone but at peace. I know in my heart of hearts and with confirmation from son, Tim, and friend, Bruce, that he is now in heaven with his mother and many of my relatives who have gone before. This has helped me through my grieving process.

I can now see so many reasons why God took Cal when he did. If Cal were going to remain in need of so much assistance, he would have hated it. He had always been so athletic and vibrant. This old age stuff had become tough on him.

Later, a family friend told me Cal had shared with her his readiness to leave all this behind and move on.

One year later, in early 2020, the world was exposed to the COVID-19 pandemic and we were all told to remain in our homes. Older adults and those with conditions similar to what Cal had suffered from were extremely vulnerable. Cal would have been an absolute nut case over what the world is currently experiencing as I finish this book!

So, all in all, the Lord knew exactly the best time for Cal to take his final breath.

A co-worker who had met Cal pointed out, "Cal's energetic personality no longer fit his older body reality." This observation has really helped me cope with losing him.

Then his primary care doctor, who knew him well, said, "He tried to be tough and strong but he had a special sweetness inside."

So, Cal, how do I miss you, let me tell you the ways …

You missed our daughter being implanted with embryos. You will miss the grandkids growing up and having kids of their own.

I miss having you there for support in the tough times. Yes, there were tough times during my breast cancer recovery, but Tim and his boys were there as my nurses. We raised great kids you and me!

I'm learning to be strong and figure things out around the house. I painted the mancave and made it into a "*wo*"mancave. I have changed the furnace filters and the carbon monoxide detector. I took the car in for oil changes and repairs. Son, Todd, helped with the dryer and a broken water heater. I cut the bushes back, weeded the front yard, and keep other things going around the house. But I miss having you to bounce stuff off of. I miss you helping me make decisions. And I miss you giving me a big hug when I need it.

My life has changed, but now I have so many stories to tell. I have published two more books, both dedicated to you. As this book comes to a conclusion, God will take it where he chooses.

I renewed old friendships, made new ones, and (until I retired) maintained my sanity by continuing to work in the most supportive workplace I have ever encountered.

Losing your spouse of almost fifty years makes you realize you probably have just thirty or so more years left yourself. Then you look back to the last thirty years to when your kids were teenagers. It puts things into real perspective! Life truly is short!

Cal, you were a good man. You changed my life. You were a really crazy guy and we had so many fun times together! I was introverted and shy when we met. You brought me out of my shell. You encouraged me to get out and speak in front of people. This has made me who I am today. You were truly a blessing throughout my entire life—even through those tough times of being such different personalities!

As we aged and faced new challenges together, hopefully I wasn't too frustrating to you. I came out of my shell through our married life and got really strong during your many health crises. Sometimes you would say I wasn't the shy, quiet girl you met and married. I think what you may have meant was that I wasn't the compliant person you expected me to continue being. I hope it wasn't too terrible for you.

You gave me a wonderful life and family. We have three loving children and we are very proud of all five of our grandchildren who are becoming productive contributors to society. In this world of absent fathers and the residual aftermath, you were a stellar, godly example of a good father.

You stuck by me through all those years of struggle with our opposite personalities.

And, Lord God, you blessed us through it all—especially when we were being selfish, sinful humans!

Life is a special event and without you, I'm missing the music you brought into my life.

Chapter Wrap-Up:

Have you recently had a loss like mine? What have you done to talk about it or heal from it?

Have you considered a grief group or counselor?

I lead support groups for women who have lost a significant other—fiancés, boyfriends, or were newly married. I'd love to chat with you about finding the help you deserve.

Chapter 19

The Lonesome Spiritual Journey

As a follower of Christ, my journey began as a lonely struggle. Cal only came to a few church services with me. He wasn't really comfortable in a church. In my early days as a believer, it was hard for me to watch other couples with the husband's arm around the shoulder or waist of his wife. Feelings of envy and hurt would well up inside me. I had a loving husband, too, but no one knew it. Though I was always at church alone, I was a happily married woman. I was not single!

I remember one Sunday, when the usher asked if I were alone. I said, "Yes," and he made some comment about fixing me up. He was just trying to be helpful, but it was a concrete demonstration of what the spouse of an unsaved person can experience at church. For years at whatever church I attended I found it difficult to *really* fit in. Oh, I'd go to the Bible studies. I'd participate. People accepted me. The problem came when everything was geared toward couples. In a way, I was kept apart from others in the church.

Others seemed to have difficulty understanding my personal pain. They couldn't know my pain, unless they'd lived it.

If you have a friend (could also be a husband whose wife doesn't know Jesus) in that situation, please reach out and show you care. Try to understand their unique pain. Christian sisters (and brothers) need one another regardless of their husband's (or wife's) spiritual condition.

In my early days as a believer, I struggled to develop a new love in my heart for Cal instead of a bitter heart of resentment. Not being able to successfully combine my two loves—my husband and my God—sometimes made my life feel very divided and definitely lonely.

I felt desperate to let people at church know I had this great, though unsaved, husband, and I wanted so badly to have him see what Christ had to offer. During my first year as a believer, before I learned what *not* to do, I tried to change Cal by leaving tracts and Bibles and stuff from various ministries all around the house, hoping against hope that he would find God through them. Not a good idea! This turned out to be just a turn-off to my unsaved spouse.

Early in my own walk, I was determined to convert Cal so I invited him on a church camping weekend. He agreed to come, so as a family we attended. Excited that this might be *the* moment of his conversion, I tried to manipulate him and control the situation instead of leaving things up to God. I told the people in charge of the campout that Cal was a professional emcee and, one night, they asked him to help with some games. As we walked toward the campfire, we heard everyone singing praise songs. You would not believe how quickly Cal turned back to our campsite! He was completely turned off and I had egg on my face for opening my big mouth. Being a pushy broad, I have had to learn the hard way too many times!

Thank goodness I eventually learned not to push my new Christian beliefs on my husband though I learned to persevere in my prayer life for his salvation by praying that "the seed" would fall on "good soil" in his heart (Luke 8:15). Sometimes, however, I prayed for this prayer more for my benefit than for his. Either way, as Gary Thomas says in his book *Sacred Influence*, "a gentle and quiet heart, mixed with a patient spirit, in a woman who keeps praying and who finds ways to connect with her husband greatly increases the possibility that she will one day pray to the God of her dreams *with* the man of her dreams."[1] My own wonderful someday came the day he was released from the hospital after his second heart attack. We prayed together for the first time. It was an exciting step.

Gradually I began to see our spiritual and communication problems in a way that helped me to understand both of us better. Over the years, we adjusted to our religious differences and Cal eventually found Messiah Jesus.

The biggest challenge in my life has been the salvation of my family. But I always held onto God's promises because he has fulfilled other promises in our lives.

> "This is the covenant I will establish with the people of Israel after that time, declares the LORD. I will put my laws in their minds and write them on their hearts. I will be their God, and they will be my people." (Hebrews 8:10)

> "And everyone who calls on the name of the LORD will be saved;" (Joel 2:32)

"But if serving the LORD seems undesirable to you, then choose for yourselves this day whom you will serve, whether the gods your ancestors served beyond the Euphrates, or the gods of the Amorites, in whose land you are living. But as for me and my household, we will serve the LORD." (Joshua 24:15)

"He will bring you a message through which you and all your household will be saved." (Acts 11:14)

"'Believe in the Lord Jesus, and you will be saved—you and your household.'" (Acts 16:31)

"For the unbelieving husband has been sanctified through his wife, and the unbelieving wife has been sanctified through her believing husband. Otherwise your children would be unclean, but as it is, they are holy." (1 Corinthians 7:14)

The kids eventually found their way to Jesus, but Cal still struggled to get on board.

Cal's faith story is hard to explain. He was very private about it. He did share that as a child his mother would say nightly prayers with him and Cal had strong faith in God, perhaps because of those prayers. I didn't always understand why Cal couldn't see the fullness of his Judaism, but he didn't like talking about it.

Messiah Jesus was simply a different concept for most of Cal's adult life. But my husband remained very tolerant and supportive of my faith despite his own struggles to believe.

Later in life, Cal said he knew Jesus, but was still uncomfortable attending church services. If he ever expressed the desire, however,

I was willing to change churches to be together with him at any church he chose. He did come to many of my small group potluck parties, so many of my church friends knew and accepted him. And once he even asked to go to church with me to thank volunteers who had helped us with yardwork the weekend before.

Cal and I never really experienced spiritual intimacy by attending church regularly, reading the Bible, or praying together. I longed for that in our marriage. But after one of his hospital stays we had an opportunity to pray a version of the Salvation Prayer together. After that, he confessed to have "a thing going with Jesus."

Cal continued his search for answers and told me Jesus was in his heart. I held onto that closely, but continued to pray that he would truly understand what having God in his heart meant. I prayed for Cal's eyes to be opened and for him to be guided to the Truth.

As time went on, our son Tim and Cal spent a lot of time together talking about the Lord. Tim strongly believed that Cal was developing a relationship with his Messiah.

Once when we were out walking, Cal suddenly stopped to pick up some folded-up bills, looking around to be sure no one was looking for it, so he could return it. When we got to our car, he counted the money—$200. The amount was exactly what we had needed for a car repair. Cal attributed this to be a direct message from God and I consider this experience a turning point in his journey to salvation and a relationship with his Messiah, Jesus.

Cal was growing in his new faith and even acknowledged Jesus as a force in his life. He would often describe his faith as half Jewish and half believer in Christ.

Over time, I saw a difference in him. He was such a good man that it was hard to notice any kind of difference, but he used less offensive language and just seemed more caring, if that were even possible. I hope and pray that he found the God of grace through his Messiah, Jesus, as he walked toward heaven.

A few days before Cal died, a good friend and his wife prayed for us. Our friend told me later, "Cal wasn't feeling well and you, Angela, and I were praying with him. I had lifted his illness up to Jesus and when I mentioned Jesus, Cal squeezed my hand twice." Our friend ended the prayer with "In Jesus' name." He says, "We all released our hands and Cal looked right at me and said 'Thank you' with his eyes and gave me a little nod and a smile. I really felt he was acknowledging the power of Jesus. It was an unspoken moment, but I really felt he knew Jesus!" With Cal's sensitivity to the name of Jesus, we were all encouraged that his relationship with the Lord Jesus might have been growing stronger.

I'm so sorry that we lost him before he could write this chapter himself!

But now only God knows the depth of Cal's relationship to his Father God and Messiah Jesus….

Chapter Wrap-Up:

Make a list of friends at church who are married to an unbeliever.

How can you encourage a fellow believer in this situation?

Have you and your significant other ever prayed together? If not, try doing so today.

When is the last time you prayed for family (and others) for salvation or a closer walk with Jesus? Consider making a list of unsaved loved ones and begin to pray for them every day.

Have you reached out for prayer or other help?

Chapter 20

Get to Know Your Husband's Family History

To understand Cal better, I had begun an exploration into our family differences to find answers that would help strengthen my marriage to Cal. Sometimes life deals us a pretty tough hand. We can be influenced by the way we were raised, our family of origin, birth order, the way people have treated us, and the expectations we put on ourselves or others put on us. A marriage consists of two very different people with very different backgrounds and personalities! I think this is why the Lord encouraged me to reflect on how we met, our families of origin, his school struggles, our birth order, our temperaments, his learning disability, and much more.

These next few chapters might encourage you to do some research too. My search increased Cal's and my understanding of one another. This was our first step to creating a successful, loving marriage.

Cal's family was not stereotypical of the American Jewish family. Socially, his parents were not in prominent positions and they were not wealthy. Cal's mother seemed less concerned about social appearances than she was about emotional, relational family connections.

Ironically, in many ways my family was socially more like the Jewish families in our community than Cal's was. Education was very important and my mother expected me to marry well. My father was a corporate attorney and my mother was an accomplished portrait artist with a master's degree in fine arts. My mother's own education was unusual for the time and she wanted no less for me.

The greatest blessing I have enjoyed from being a part of Cal's wonderfully close-knit, family is their sense of family. They showed me how to have a close family. My desire to join an ethnic family through our intercultural marriage turned out to be a good choice. I learned what Genesis 2:24 meant firsthand by leaving my father's home to become one flesh with my husband. This has given me the freedom to grow into the woman of God he wants me to be … but it has not been easy.

Cal's entire family of birth still live within minutes of each other. Julie has kept in touch with her female cousins. Cal's mother, Claire, certainly set a wonderful example in family togetherness and being there for each other. My husband's family became my own just like Naomi's did for Ruth in the Bible. In fact, my Jewish name upon conversion was Ruth and Ruth 1:16 will be the Scripture engraved on my tombstone.

Several years ago, Tim, his wife, and their first child, Jeremiah, were driving through New York State from California. When they called to tell my parents that they would be in the area, rather than inviting them to stay at their house, my mother seemed to be rushed helping my brother prepare for a trade show. My mother was concerned that their baby might cry and disturb my brother prior to the show. In contrast, Cal's mother would have dropped everything to be with her little "Bubala" Jeremiah.

With the Lord's help, I have been able to take the good things of my upbringing and combine them with the family values and warmth Cal's mother possessed. I found that Cal and I combined the good things we experienced in our families of origin and were able to make our own developing family better. We have a legacy of a great nuclear family to show for it. Through our example, the kids grew healthy, close-knit families of their own. However, it was very hard for Cal to release Tim and his family when they moved to Hawaii to be close to his wife's family. Cal had always thought the kids would live close to us.

Initially, Julie and Michael chose to live in Julie's California home rather than move to Michael's home in Dallas. I think Cal was a large part of that decision for them. Now, that he's gone, they may move out of state.

Cal's perspective of his upbringing was sometimes negative. He remembered and sometimes focused on childhood pain, especially in academic struggles with educators who only understood kids who fit neatly inside their academic boxes. Cal occasionally used to share a bad summer camp experience he had at a military-style summer camp. Unfortunately, that camp experience made Cal very homesick and created travel problems for us later. He wasn't comfortable venturing very far from home.

As time went on, his developing health problems removed his ability to enjoy traveling for fear that something would go wrong. This was a big difference between us, since I loved to travel and had at one time wanted to be a flight attendant. I love to go to new places. Ironically, he loved to explore new places too, however, being far from home or stuck without a car stressed him out. Our road trip vacations became a good compromise.

Eventually, Cal overcame claustrophobia as it related to flying in an airplane. The cruise his family treated us to gave him the tools that helped him learn to cope. This was a great example of how his birth family always pulled together.

It started when they pulled together for us during one of Cal's early health scares. They could see how stressed I was and his brother's wife, Jan, who had lost a husband to a long illness understood my need to get away. Together they decided to make the cruise happen for us. Since Cal was claustrophobic, he wasn't sure about going until his brother-in-law, a psychiatrist, assured him he could have whatever drugs he needed in order to relax. We all laughed at the idea that we could just knock him out for the entire trip!

As it turned out, he never took the meds and was able to cope beyond his own expectations. That led to his decision to join the family in visiting my parents for their birthdays. He ended up loving his flight experience as he had in the past.

A lot of the credit goes to Julie who researched and selected the best possible airline and flight schedule to maximize his comfort. Thanks to her efforts, Cal began to have the courage to try other trips. My desire to travel became possible again.

Cal also shared some of his mother's fears. He learned to swim late in life because his mother was afraid of the water. When he came home from college with a small motorcycle, his mother hit the roof! His mother's fears were passed down in a similar situation when our adult son, Tim started riding a motorcycle. Cal was afraid something would happen to him.

When our fathers were raising us, fathers were not particularly involved in their children's lives until they entered school or got involved in sports, in the case of boys. This has changed today. I see this as a great trend. Our boys are now "permitted" by society to be involved with their children even from a very early age. Cal would certainly have been more involved with our kids from infancy if society had encouraged it at the time.

Cal's dad was a kind man, but for the most part was much quieter and more reserved than Cal. Cal clearly took after his mother with her fiery, emotional personality.

His older brother and sister suggested that their family might all have been affected by their parent's experience during the Great Depression. They were clearly exposed to the dangers of running out of money, while my parents seemed to have been affected less severely. This seems to have made his family fearful of taking on any financial risks, while mine, though cautious about money, were not fearful in their approach to it as they aged.

This probably made Cal's bouts of unemployment even more scary to him.

Chapter Wrap-Up:

If you have not already done so, consider having a conversation with your spouse about their upbringing. Make note of differences and similarities and then determine how best to blend each for your family.

Chapter 21

Get to know your Husband's Position in his Family

Since Cal is a youngest child and I am the eldest, I thought I'd explore these differences to see if that could help us understand each other better.

I found *The Birth Order Book* by Dr. Kevin Leman really helpful.

First, I discovered that in terms of birth order we were the perfect couple—an oldest child and the baby of the family. It just made sense. As the oldest child, I was used to taking control and Cal was used to being told what to do.

Sounds great, until I examined it from Cal's point of view during his unemployment mid-life crisis. His life was out of control. He needed something to do. Being home and out of work made him feel the need to take control of something—anything! Unfortunately, I resented his interference in household matters. That was *my* place, *my* domain. My stupid ego kept flaring up! To complicate things, as I grew in business knowledge and expertise, he was made to feel less capable—like the youngest child again, the one who was too young to do it and not as accomplished as his older brother and sister.

To the family baby, "the older kids always seem to be so smart—so authoritative and knowing."[1] Those insecurities were probably coming back to haunt him.

But praise the Lord, I was led to *The Birth Order Book* just in time. It helped me understand his need to control and my need to back off. The author's insights helped me understand Cal's dominance in conversations, where he needed to be the center of attention like the baby brother he had once been. Over the years his being the center of attention was fun for me. I sort of fed off the idea that he was *my* husband. I was proud of him. I guess some babies of the family can be obnoxious. Cal never was. Not to me anyway! He had taught himself to play the guitar and always played at parties in high school. I was proud that this talented man was *mine*. He loved to emcee events and went on to do this professionally. His dream had always been to be a game show host. We even produced a single's game show for TV back in the day. The fame never came, but it was great to think he might have become famous.

However, as his self-esteem faltered, the insecurities of being the youngest child began to surface. As Dr. Leman points out, last borns are "acutely aware (that) they are youngest, smallest, weakest, and least equipped with life."[2]

Last borns tend to be people persons. This became particularly difficult when Cal was faced with unemployment. He felt isolated and alone at home. He had no audience. And with his disability in retirement, it was important for me to encourage him to get out every day to be around people. For a while he was one of the "grumpy old men" at the local Starbucks but even going to the store gave him the opportunity to share the three jokes he knew with everyone! This helped his self-esteem in old age and gave him something to do as I continued in my career.

I'm the oldest of three. As a first born, I tended to be "perfectionistic, reliable, conscientious, list maker, well-organized, critical, serious, scholarly." Cal, the last born, tended to be, "manipulative, charming, (blaming of others), (a show) off, people person, good salesperson, precocious, engaging."[3]

A great combination, but I sometimes wished that he were the wife and I was the husband. I mean, as the wife I wish I were the baby—ready for my husband to take care of me. It would have kept me out of trouble, but then I wouldn't have anything to write about! Actually, we really did balance each other perfectly in our birth order tendencies.

Cal was the child who loved his parents purely. He didn't find fault in the way they raised him, except maybe the summer they sent him off to that military-style camp! Cal was the innocent child who didn't search deeply into things for hidden meanings. He accepted things and people for their surface value, unless they caused him pain. He used to be very forgiving, but as life went on and he faced many hurts, he began holding grudges. Life was tough!

Chapter Wrap-Up:

How do you think birth order is affecting your relationship?

(Just for fun…) Have you ever thought about what it must have been like to be a sibling of Jesus?

"Accept one another, then, just as Christ accepted you, in order to bring praise to God." (Romans 15:7)

Chapter 22

Get to Know Your Husband's Education and Career Background

Financial struggles caused by Cal's occasional unemployment brought out characteristics in both of us that I needed to understand more fully. It became the first time in our relationship that our vows to stick it out "for better or for worse" became real.

I began evaluating his educational experiences.

Elementary school brought mostly Cs and Ds for Cal. High school was only slightly better, continuing with a C average in mid-level academic classes. He was not consistent in test taking either. While he scored in the third percentile from the bottom on his SATs, he seemed to learn how to successfully take the New York State Regents exams, scoring high in both Chemistry and Physics. On the other hand, he was an accomplished gymnast and a competitive athlete in high school. The first of his natural abilities to be attacked during his career was this competitive nature. Over the years his athletic and physical abilities were challenged more than once.

His professional career began with a guidance counselor telling him he should pursue his education at a trade school, rather than attend college. But he desperately desired a college education because both of his siblings had PhDs. The Vietnam War was looming and college offered some protection from the draft. Starting at a community college, he struggled through his first two years of college. He almost gave up, getting 4 Ds and 1 C during his first semester. However, planning our marriage seemed to help him to look forward to a new phase in his life.

Moving into his major at a four-year college, he learned to pattern himself after successful students. This helped him to eventually graduate Dean's List. He never really investigated careers that he might want to pursue—he simply majored in Psychology and Elementary Education since that was what his brother and sister had done. Teaching appeared to be a respectable profession.

Following graduation, he began interviewing for teaching positions, but was continually rejected. When he was being considered for an excellent local school district, he didn't want to blow it again and identified a question that was always asked during the interview process. Knowing he must be doing something wrong, he went back to the Dean of Students at college to get her advice.

He had been continually asked, "Mr. Gormick, what do you consider to be your greatest weakness as a teacher?" Since he had only student taught, he responded something indicating his lack of teaching experience during one interview. Since reading was not a strong point, he had answered, "I suppose reading," at another. Not wanting to blow it again, the dean gave him an ideal response.

"Perhaps it would be better to indicate your lack of experience in dealing with individual differences."

He couldn't wait to try this astute answer! But he knew he had to time his response just so. Holding back, he knew the question would come. He could hardly contain himself!

Finally, the principal asked, "Mr. Gormick, what do you consider to be your greatest weakness as a teacher?"

He held his breath, appearing to think through for the best answer and, a moment later, he confidently stated, "Perhaps it would be that I lack experience in dealing with individual differences."

The principal was so impressed with this answer that he immediately took him into the superintendent's office and hired Cal on the spot. Excited, he came home to share the good news with me. We began planning our long-awaited family and Todd was born the following June—nine months to the day after he started as a fourth-grade teacher.

He only taught for one year, though, before deciding we would join the rest of his family in California. His first year of teaching had been tough because he was never taught how to do lesson plans in college and his fellow teachers seemed unsupportive. He would have been a great teacher had he received a little more encouragement. He gravitated to the kids who were struggling in school the way he had. However, being in a fourth-grade classroom actually brought back some of Cal's own insecurities from school.

Teaching jobs were hard to come by in California. They had more teachers than open teaching jobs. From New York, we sent résumé after résumé to California school districts to no avail. We were determined to move there to join his family, so with our newborn son and our cat, we packed up our station wagon and pioneered our way to California figuring we would stay as long as we could until Cal got a job.

Upon our arrival to California, he used an executive search firm to find a job at the regional office of an insurance company. Positions in the insurance field carried prestige. He'd learned that in a psychology class he took. Back then, insurance positions topped the list of prestigious careers followed by the legal profession and teaching. He had the desire to become the president of an insurance company and he wanted to follow the correct career track for his family.

During the interview process, he had to get the approval of the managers of ten departments in order to be hired. Again, he used his natural sales ability and rapport-building skills. He developed points of sale and gave each manager the exact words they wanted to hear. He used to admit that he, unknowingly, set himself up for an extremely low point in his career life. He got the job but within a very short time had failed miserably at administration. He believed the experience had been a big mistake.

He had been responsible for managing twenty-five people through his knowledge of all aspects and procedures of insurance, things he had learned working his way through college at an insurance company. He also had to possess good management qualities. But many of those he managed were resentful that this young upstart had gotten the job and they hadn't. On top of that, he knew he would be totally incapable of firing people. He felt humiliated in front of all ten departments when he was let go.

Due to these setbacks early in his career, he felt he would never be any good at anything. He had no confidence in the things he did.

Old feelings of failure as a kid in school surfaced. He felt awful because he had a growing family relying on him. What he didn't realize was he had been a product of circumstances rather than making his own proactive choices.

After this disheartening set of events, he noticed a little office across the street from the insurance company. It was the Boy Scouts of America headquarters. As a former Explorer Scout leader while in college, he had heard about the professional side of scouting—a career involving kids and offering prestige.

With this new job, he found a way to have the prestige he longed for and hoped to facilitate a move into an executive career. Again, he built rapport with people and presented the professional image they were looking for. The position didn't pay much and he worked long hours, but he knew this would help him to advance within Corporate America. He learned how to speak in front of audiences, manage objectives, set goals, delegate responsibilities, train volunteers, and administrate thousands of kids, families, and volunteers. He loved the job and his career progressed well.

Following a successful three-year stint with the BSA, he felt ready to move into the corporate arena and make more money. Offered an opportunity to return to the field of insurance in a sales position, he left scouting and began down a path that was to prove to be another wrong turn. He quickly discovered that selling life insurance was *not* the right path for him! Fortunately, he was back on the right track within a month when he entered the field of title insurance. He spent four years in that industry, utilizing the people skills he had developed within the Boy Scout program. He loved working closely with realtors, helping to make them more successful.

From there he advanced into the banking field and discovered a whole new world in which to use his people skills and marketing abilities. He wasn't required to be a detail person. He was the door opener. He had finally found his prestigious professional career position in banking. Subsequently, he switched industries, successfully moving through banking to venture capital and, later, into commercial real estate development.

Fifteen years after finding his career niche, the economy took a turn for the worse, and he was out pounding the pavement once again. It took him a long time to find employment this time and, even then, in the interest of his family, he settled for a position that promised to allow him to make presentations on behalf of the company as the program grew. That was not to be and he remained stuck behind a computer for a couple of years. One day, frustrated and unable to cope any longer, he gave his notice and left without another job lined up.

After many months of searching for another job, frustration and depression shut him down.

At some point we had taken Gary Smalley and Dr. John Trent's Personality Inventory, which is based on characteristics demonstrated by four different animals: Lions, Otters, Golden Retrievers, and Beavers.[1]

Cal scored predominately in the Otter classification. Otters tend to be fun-loving, entertainers, enthusiastic motivators, creative, verbal, relaxed by being with people, and they love to talk. My main personality related to the Lion, which exhibits leadership qualities. Lions are take-charge, visionary, sometimes intimidating people.

Not surprisingly, too much of this quality can create a problem in personal relationships, like marriage. Duh! As you will soon see, that was me every time I turned around—causing relationship issues.

In any event, with Cal feeling so frustrated and depressed, we sat down to talk. Our kids were almost grown, so accepting and acknowledging my leadership qualities (above), my choleric personality (described in the next chapter), and my oldest child family position, we decided I was ready to work full-time again. I encouraged Cal to expand our fundraising company and start doing professional emceeing, thus acknowledging his Otter-type personality, his youngest child need for attention, and his desire to be the center of attention. He loved being in front of audiences and he was good at it.

Somewhere along the way he tried to become a television game show host. It was fun at times, but soon became a demoralizing disappointment that seemed to set him back into the place where his childhood insecurities surfaced once again.

Slowly he recovered and took on a major nonprofit client emceeing their celebrity dinner events. He was able to do this for about three years before his health began to deteriorate.

During Cal's long struggles through career disappointments and unemployment, our relationship struggled as well. We lost heart, as many do, when our relationship was strained. Marriage difficulties shake us up the most.

We were not the same happy-go-lucky couple from twenty years prior. Each of us had become a different person. The difficulties of life seemed to have brought out the worst in each of us. This only amplified our differences, especially in the area of our individual coping mechanisms. We were both broken people!

I had more to explore.

Chapter Wrap-Up:

How has your school experience colored your later life?

How has your spouse's school experience colored their life?

What work experiences do each of you share? Or are you complete opposites?

Take the Gary Smalley Personality Types Inventory and seek to find common ground.

Chapter 23

Get to Know Yourselves as a Couple - What is Your Personality Temperment?

In studying our families of origin, birth orders and Cal's school and career experiences, I was beginning to understand us better as a couple—the way we could effectively face life as a team. Some answers began to become evident, when I picked up a copy of Beverly LaHaye's *The Spirit-Controlled Woman* to study our differing temperaments.

I knew it was the Spirit that would make the difference, but I'd given myself to the Holy Spirit before. I'd ask him to guide my life. I'd pray for Holy Spirit words in situations where I was afraid my old self might take over, but it wasn't until I read LaHaye's book that things began to fall into place. Her discussions of the four basic temperaments began coming back to me. I'd heard about them before, but not from her perspective and not with the open heart I had finally developed. LaHaye is known for holding onto traditional values, the values that I knew were right even for the godly woman of the 1990s (and now for the twenty-first century.) Her book provided a wealth of information.

Upon taking her temperament test, I discovered I was a combination of the Choleric and Sanguine temperaments. Her book provided the following facts: Cholerics are often business owners. "Choleric wives often struggle with the biblical role of submission ... Many Spirit-filled Cholerics have learned wifely submission out of obedience to the Lord."[1]

Even the Sanguine side of my personality was an issue. The outgoing, life of the party aspects were sometimes in conflict with Cal's need to be the center of attention. Sometimes I would come on too strong for Cal.

Searching for my temperament was not only fun, it changed my life!

LaHaye advised that Cholerics must do the following: "Walk in the Spirit and seek to do God's will and not theirs *day by day* (my emphasis). Gain victory over their lifetime battle with the harmful emotion of anger and replace it with love, joy, and peace from the Holy Spirit."[2]

Clearly, this is an on-going lifetime, spiritual battle for me! Praise God that anger has not been a major difficulty for me. I think, however, during the years of Cal's unemployment (and later during his declining health) that I was experiencing hidden anger. I would get so frustrated!

LaHaye's book helped me understand that my temperament was contributing to this lifetime struggle. That's why I felt as if I were always slipping. Eventually, I began feeling a little better as I discovered God's version of me.

As a female believer in Christ with a Choleric Temperament I had some great strengths, but also had some pretty heavy weaknesses to overcome. The positive characteristics I identified included my confidence and natural leadership ability, strong-willed, self-determined attitudes, optimism, and self-sufficiency.

Those are great traits for success in the world, but I'm not of this world—I'm a follower of Christ and my husband was my head.

Difficulties involving my lack of compassion coupled with a tendency to make decisions for Cal didn't support his male headship. It depleted it!

LaHaye suggests that the Choleric "needs to become sensitive to the needs of others and to develop her inner beauty by spending quiet hours reading the Bible and praying."[3] I believe the Lord circumcised my heart as he took me through the Word. That made such a difference.

LaHaye explains that my Sanguine Temperament softens my Choleric side as a ChlorSan. Praise the Lord! My Sanguine side makes me "warm and lively; charismatic and talkative." I am an "infectious conversationalist with an unusual capacity for enjoyment."[4] However, my weaknesses of restlessness and coming on too strong (to Cal) were not helpful during his times of struggle.

These weaknesses, when things were going well for Cal, could usually be overlooked. But they became potentially dangerous to our marriage, given his middle-aged, crazy emotional state. There really is such a thing! Unemployed men face severe ego deflation. Way back in the time of Adam and Eve, God created man to be the provider for his family. Men doubt themselves when they are failing to provide. Insecurity surfaces concerning their male leadership capabilities. Failure is their greatest fear. Cal knew he was responsible for "the financial security of his family." He was also supposed to "provide the emotional security needed by both his wife and his children."[5] My opinionated nature, and insensitivity to his needs did not help me to bring him good not harm as it says in Proverbs 31:12.

If I weren't too insensitive and if he weren't hurting too much, then my temperament strengths added to our relationship. Otherwise, our relationship was in trouble.

LaHaye warns that the ChlorSan, "is so powerful that … it is often hard to tell whether she is speaking on behalf of her will or God's. ChlorSans need humbling, which usually takes a series of tribulations and frustrating experiences before they genuinely learn to lean on God."[6] I have certainly had my share of that.

The fact that I am a strong leader was *not* a positive characteristic for us. I couldn't be myself and when my natural self came out, even if controlled by the Spirit, it would threaten Cal.

My Sanguine side, in social settings, became hurtful to him. He'd accuse me of dominating the conversation in group settings and, admittedly, I usually did dialog about the business I had started.

I'm a good organizer, decisive, have a capacity for action, don't vacillate, am very practical, can stimulate others to action, and I set goals. During Cal's times of unemployment, these good things were making me crazy! I knew what I wanted, how to do it and, honestly, if I were not operating out of the home office, with Cal's many interruptions, I would have been much more productive.

Additional confirmations came as I prepared and taught a Bible study based on *The Confident Woman*. I learned more about personalities within self-destructive marriages. I wouldn't really call ours a self-destructive relationship, but, at times, it was sure close, given our particular circumstances. Clarification of the "dominant woman" married to the "threatened macho male" could easily have described us. I just praise the Lord that God directed me in his paths of change even before I came across Gillham's Bible study.

Chapter Wrap-Up:

There are any number of personality or temperament tests online. Many are at no cost. Try one with your spouse to get a better understanding of your personalities and temperaments.

Chapter 24

Get to Know Yourselves as a Couple – Love Styles

I continued to explore relationship books and came across *How We Love* by Milan and Kay Yerkovich. Their book helped me examine our love styles resulting from emotional attention or lack thereof within each of our birth homes.

As the authors explain, "Our experiences growing up, good and bad, (leave) a lasting imprint in our souls that determine our beliefs and expectations about how to give and receive love … All of us have an imprint of intimacy, the sum of our learning how to love. Our imprint determines our love style—how we interact with others when it comes to love."[1]

They go on to explain Attachment Theory. "Attachment Theory, simply put, is based on a child's bond with his or her primary caregiver. God designed us to need connection, and our relationships with our parents is the first place this happens—or doesn't happen. Attachment Theory outlines specifically what can go wrong and looks at how our ability to love is shaped by our first experiences with our parents and caregivers during our early years. These early experiences leave a lasting imprint on our souls that is still observable in our adult relationships."[2]

"If your parents had difficulty noticing and soothing your distress, you probably grew up in a family with little emotional connection."[3] That sounded like my home of origin for sure!

"There are five harmful love styles: the avoider, pleaser, vacillator, controller and victim." These love styles "… all grow out of a childhood reaction to anxiety prompted by a lack of comfort, affection, and emotional connection."[4]

Cal and I took the Yerkovich's Love Style Quiz to evaluate possible harmful love styles in our relationship.

It seems that I am an Avoider and Cal was a Vacillator based on the quiz. Probably, since emotions were not encouraged in my home, I tested as an Avoider. Avoiders tend to be very independent and are often driven type-A personalities who can become workaholics. Well, that sounds like me!

Avoiders "… learned early on to minimize their feelings, be independent, and meet their own needs."[5] Characteristics of Avoiders, which I have, are self-sufficiency and task-oriented high achievement. Controller characteristics I have include the fact that I was angered and stressed by my parents growing up, I tend to stay in the present a lot, but I do think about the past though I don't dwell in the past, and I wished Cal would have heard me out more.[6]

Cal apparently longed for closer connections in relationships and had high expectations of those around him but found people often let him down. That made him a Vacillator. "Vacillators found out early on that connection was sometimes available but unpredictable, and these kids were often left waiting, so by the time attention was offered, they were too angry to receive it."[7]

Cal exhibited Vacillator characteristics like being easily disappointed and rejected, and becoming angry when his expectations weren't met. At times, I felt like I had to walk on eggshells around him. He had trouble accepting the weaknesses of others (accepting them for who they are.) He sometimes felt angry rather than sad over his disappointment with others, and he tended to reflect more on how others had hurt him than on his own short comings.

Vacillators come from home environments of inconsistency. Abandonment is a big thing in these households, but to my knowledge his parents never left each other or abandoned the family physically. His dad did seem to be somewhat detached, but I always thought that was more a result of the times we grew up in. His mom had that fiery temper. Maybe there was something inconsistent for Cal there—never knowing if she was in a good or bad mood?

On a lighter note, Cal and I took other love style quizzes too and found other interesting results. I encourage you to find one of the free ones online.

Overall, my results indicated that I'm logical, unselfish, and best friend relationships work best for me. I am practical as I approach love relationships. Money, religion, and values influence my feelings. This might have been different when Cal and I met because we were only seventeen. We took these tests after years of marriage.

We both came out as givers, which is probably a reason why our loving relationship lasted so long. Givers are unselfish. Their needs come second to those of their loved one. Givers assume the best in their partner and focus on nurturing, kindness, and sacrifice.

In addition, I've always thought that the best love relationships were between best friends and this component proved true for us. Caring for and working together over time builds lasting bonds in relationship and feelings of deep affection. Surely, this was what got us through the hardest of times.

Cal's love style was one of a more "Possessive Relationship." Being together was important to him. Honestly I didn't like other characteristics of the Possessive Relationship like being "anxious" if the partner isn't near; jealousy and obsession. None of those were ever a problem with Cal, but as we analyzed this further, his lack of selfishness and the giver component prevented serious issues typically found in this type of relationship.

I came into the marriage from a logical approach, while Cal came from a more emotional focus. I think those differences balanced us to create a good team through life.

Chapter Wrap-Up:

Have you ever explored how you love one another and why?

Did either or both of you experience a childhood trauma? If so, how has it impacted your relationship?

Chapter 25

News Flash! Males and Females View Marriage Differently

From here I decided to explore some basic differences between males and females as it pertained to marriage. Maybe I was having trouble understanding Cal because of that.

Thomas confirmed it. He shares "that many, if not most, problems in marriage crop up, not between two individuals, but between two genders."[1] There it was! I needed to understand Cal's guy side better.

Thomas continues, "Men's brains also need to 'rest' more than women's, with the result that men are more inclined to seek 'mental naps.' Why do men gravitate toward the television screen and then launch through the channels instead of focusing on one program? … At the end of the day, we don't want plot, story, or character development; we just want escape (think buildings blowing up, cars crashing, tires squealing). All the while, *your* brain—which has fifteen percent more blood flow—is still running late in the day and therefore better able to process complex entertainment."[2]

And I thought Cal jumped from one channel to another because of his Attention Deficit Disorder! It was just because he was a guy!

In John Gray's book, *Men Are From Mars Women Are From Venus*, I found something that helped us.

Cal sometimes resisted my suggestions on things or referrals to someone who could help him. As Gray explained, it makes a woman feel "as though he doesn't care; she feels her needs are not being respected. As a result, she understandably feels unsupported and stops trusting him.

Admittedly, I might have given him "unsolicited advice or criticism."[3]

This caused problems because Cal's reaction was like that of other men. "I don't like it when she starts telling me how I should do things. I don't feel admired. Instead, I feel like I'm being treated like a child. He needs to feel admired. Instead, he feels put down."[4]

Not understanding this can result in arguments, which could be avoided by identifying and fulfilling the husband's primary emotional needs.

And what are those needs?

Gray explains that "men need to receive trust, acceptance, appreciation, admiration, approval and encouragement."[5]

Sometimes I may have failed to trust Cal to make the right decision. But when I tried to help him solve a problem, his struggle with accepting my help frustrated me. I felt like he wasn't hearing me or respecting my opinion.

Reading more about gender differences and possible solutions helped us to understand each other better. It was extremely helpful and created better communication between us overall.

Successful marriages are certainly based on frequent, effective, clear, and open communication along with saying "I love you." We also need to feel appreciated, make time for each other as a couple, and have separate time for our own interests. It's important to agree to disagree, build trust, and learn to forgive. Words and advice to live by, but not always easy for us.

Chapter Wrap-Up:

How often do you say "I love you"?

Do you and your husband ask for forgiveness?

What communication methods do you use as a couple?

How do you each argue?

Chapter 26

Get to Know Your Own Differences as Individuals

Besides the male female thing, how different were we anyway? How opposite? Let me count the ways!

Cal tended to be very impatient, while I can be very patient, almost to a fault.

He was innately compassionate. Though I care deeply about people, it takes me longer to be empathetic and understanding of the needs of others. I tend to go into solutions as a problem solver, before being just a good listener. For instance, Cal would think about what would make the cats more comfortable or give them something to play with. I loved them but figured they were just animals and wouldn't notice the difference anyway. Actually, he was a dog lover and I'm a cat lover. The reason I prefer cats is that they aren't as dependent as dogs are. They are good companions, but are a lot less work. I don't know if that reflects a lack of compassion, but that's just the way I am! In fact, when I lost both cats (in the same year I lost Cal), I had no need to replace them even though it made the whole house much lonelier.

Cal developed serious health problems. Even as a senior and a breast cancer survivor, I am extremely healthy. My mom lived to be eighty-nine and my dad to be ninety-five, though Dad did develop dementia.

Cal's mother died at the age of sixty-three. That was very hard on Cal. Watching his father fade away of heart disease was no easier.

Cal tended to be a pessimist though he disguised it well early in our relationship! I am very optimistic. I think I got my optimism from my dad who, though he was a WWII prisoner of war, knew he would make it home from the war.

Cal was an accomplished singer. I would clear the room if I sang! His recordings from karaoke singing really helped me through my grief period during my first year without him.

Cal always asked for directions when we were lost. I would never admit we were lost until we'd exhausted every possibility.

When we would eat meat, Cal had his meat cooked medium well and mine was always rare. I love Blue Cheese, Feta, and Parmesan. You'd think he would die if he even smelled any of them!

That brings us to his ability to smell. You'd think olfactory senses would decline with age. No such luck! He smelled everything and complained about it every time.

I looked forward to cuddling and sleeping under the same covers when we were married, but he insisted from our honeymoon night on that he had to have his own set of covers.

I love it cold at night. He had to have it warm. He preferred the A/C and I liked to have the window open at night. (Although this was great when I experienced my age-related menopause night sweats.)

I love camping and Cal had to have the luxuries of home if we even attempted that form of recreation.

I am a prodigal daughter, while he was a faithful son.

He was spontaneous and I must plan things out.

When communicating, we were alike in our comfort level with bickering. However, our reactions were significantly different in serious couple communications. Cal seemed to want to change the subject and cut off the discussion as soon as he felt uncomfortable. I needed to get all my feelings and thoughts out before I felt fully heard—probably a male/female thing.

As frustrating as Cal and I being exact opposites in so many things was, he was truly my other half. As such, Cal completed me and I completed him. In many ways, he needed to be my opposite to fill in the gaps of my weaknesses and strengths and vice versa. He always made me laugh. He made me a better person for knowing him.

It is important to clarify that we survived as a couple because our life values were the same. On the important things we either agreed or I was eventually able to back down in deference to his position as head of household. (It's that yielding thing again!) We believed the same things in raising our children. We agreed on money issues most of the time, though as we saved for retirement I wished he were more of a risk-taker. I desire to trust God more for his provision, but I was afraid Cal was more like the servant in Matthew 25:14–18 . Cal chose to keep a bulk of our money in CDs which—since the Great Economic Crash of 2008–2010—didn't provide much interest at all. But I must admit that during that crash we didn't lose anything because none of our money, at the time, was in stocks or mutual funds. So, I may be doing better than others because Cal was so conservative. We agreed on ways to save money and I even wrote a book about it. We both prided ourselves on being on time for things.

For what it's worth, we used to enjoy bowling together. In the end, we couldn't bowl together due to his declining health, but our love and relationship continued until his death. We just loved being together!

There is never a guaranteed security that a marriage will last, whether the couple marries young or when they are more mature. Our early expectations were of having fun and being best friends. Of course, that was very simplistic and somewhat immature. We learned quickly to decide we had to make a lifelong commitment to one another.

I grew to love my husband more deeply through this research phase of my journey and it has prepared me to be a better partner in my new relationships.

Chapter Wrap-Up:

How has my story made you start thinking about your own relationships?

Do you have date nights to get away together? How about weekends away without the kids? If not, write down some ideas about how you could schedule some time with your spouse.

Chapter 27

Beware of Insecurities and Destructive Coping Mechanisms

Much appears in media about abusive families, dysfunctional families, and unhealthy environments. Personally, I believe that all families are dysfunctional in one way or another, at one time or another. Parents aren't even the same people as each child enters the family unit. Overprotective with the first child, they can become too relaxed with their third.

I think that personality differences and other factors can affect the child's reactions to being in a dysfunctional family regardless of what that dysfunction might be. My brother identifies as a highly sensitive person (HSP) and he is a peacemaker while I'm a rebel. So, our individual reactions to the dysfunction are very different.

Negative emotions and feelings were discouraged in my family of origin. Therefore, I explored codependency, which can occur in dysfunctional homes. But if either of our family of origins suffered from codependency, Cal and I seemed unaffected.

Codependency is a learned behavior, but as "Givers" on our mutual personality tests, we didn't exhibit any of the typical characteristics found in codependent households. However, in working through issues you might be experiencing in your relationship, it may be valuable for you to explore this too. Though usually found in homes with addiction present, the concept of codependency can sometimes be applied to other situations where drug or alcohol use is not present. Therefore, if you or your spouse grew up in the home of an addict or you suffered a childhood trauma, you might want to explore codependency as it could seriously affect all your future relationships.

Cal and I came from distinctly different backgrounds.

While we lived in the nicest part of town, Cal was from the "other side of the tracks." He was Jewish and we were Episcopalian (even though I didn't accept that faith as my own.) He grew up in a culturally Jewish home. My ancestors have been in this country since at least the Revolutionary War and can be traced back several generations to England and Ireland. (Big whoop!)

I think I was never ready to live in my birth family. I always felt I was a misfit for that family of rules, structures, perfection, etc. I wanted to belong to a "real" family with real emotions and not so many false pretenses of portraying a proper image to the outside world. In my family of origin, social norms were to be kept up no matter what.

So often we marry someone just like our own mother or father, but I didn't want a relationship like my parents'. I saw in Cal a strength I didn't see in my own father who was a more passive male. That strength attracted me to him.

Mistakenly, I didn't see a passion of love in my parents' relationship. It seemed to be commitment without passion. Recently, however, I found a poem my mother wrote about my dad back when they were dating. There was passion there, at least in their early years together. Oh, how I wish they'd been more demonstratively affectionate when I was growing up. Unfortunately, I think phony, societal acceptability prevented that. I'd rather think that, than think the years had taken away their passion.

Because they were reserved and proper, my mother, a dominant female, was always in control. Dad was successful in business, as an attorney and the department head for a major automobile manufacturer. At home, however, he was dominated and subtly manipulated by my mother. I didn't want that to happen to me and Cal. I sensed my own tendency toward being a dominant female, desiring to be in control.

Eve's curse, discussed in John and Stasi Eldredge's book *Captivating: Unveiling the Mystery of a Woman's Soul* explains more. As Eve's daughter, both my mother and I had "the urge to control." Eldredge further explains, "Women dominate and control because they fear their vulnerability."[1]

I'd never considered that idea before. I project an image of strength. I take control to avoid issues that could arise. It's what makes me a good manager.

But I think that I probably feel the need to be in control because I had vulnerable, painful feelings from a lack of control during childhood. I believe that being in control as an adult has been my attempt to protect myself from the fear of what others thought of me or being judged for my imperfections. I wasn't trusting God. And God told me so.

"So we say in confidence, 'The Lord is my helper; I will not be afraid. What can mere mortals do to me?'" (Hebrews 13:6)

"In God, whose word I praise—in God I trust and am not afraid. What can mere mortals do to me?" (Psalm 56:4)

"The LORD is with me; I will not be afraid. What can mere mortals do to me?" (Psalm 118:6)

It is often easy to forget this in the middle of a crisis, but God's Word *always* speaks Truth! Unfortunately, I have often feared man more than I have reverenced God. Yet another lesson for me to learn from my journey of failed career moves.

I have been able to gradually replace the fear with hope—God's hope. As I trust him for the outcome, my need to control diminishes and so does my fear of mere mortals.

I eventually developed a new understanding of my family dynamics. Apparently my mother was forced to react to my father with control because his own mother was very domineering. My mother once explained, "It was the only way she could get him to listen to her." It doesn't make it right, but knowing this information helped me understand my mother and appreciate my own husband better. And I felt blessed that Cal wasn't as passive. And he certainly possessed the passion I longed for.

He never let me get away with much. Praise God!

However, Cal's emotional instability, his ups and downs, became unpredictable. I'm sure, overall, he appreciated that I didn't become discouraged or intimidated by the circumstances. Yet sometimes he told me I didn't seem to care that we might lose the house, that there wasn't enough money to pay the bills, etc. Honestly, in all these things, I simply trusted God. While Cal lived in fear, I lived life in peace. I sometimes got uptight, but I didn't really *worry*. And he would think I didn't care! This is where the fact that he didn't know the Lord made such a big difference. Had things been different, at least we'd be coming from spiritually similar ground. I couldn't even show him biblical promises for genuine encouragement. He would call that preaching! I was caught in the middle, no matter what I said or did.

I have realized that, as a follower of Christ, sometimes I have struggled to back off in the strength of my own personality in my quest to be a respectfully, yielding wife. Unfortunately, our life had changed. The sparse 1990s were no longer the affluent 1980s. Cal's bout with unemployment had allowed his insecurities to surface, while my own strength was renewed. This was a bad, destructive, potentially lethal combination for our relationship.

My practical human side told me that *somebody* had to make the money when his income stopped.

I was always caught in the middle. However, I was also responsible for putting myself in that situation. Had I fully trusted the Lord for our provision, I wouldn't have been so fearful.

But I had many fears. Where did I find my security? Was it Cal's ability to earn a living or his commitment to stay married to me? I didn't fully understand or trust Philippians 4:19 at the time: "And my God will meet all your needs according to the riches of his glory in Christ Jesus."

Cal would say he wanted me to get a good paying job, so it wasn't his ego speaking there. But, the "women's libber" or "killer entrepreneur," "go-getter" attitude that I had could arise as a major problem to our relationship at any moment! I am truly a recovering Choleric personality!

Gillham explains in *The Confident Woman* another character flaw of mine. As many women do, I operate on "performance-based acceptance." It took me years to discover that God was the only one I needed to please and that God was pleased with me just for who I was, not for what I did. There's a big difference between having a performance-based relationship with God (the old covenant) or the grace-based relationship we can now have because the death of Jesus allowed a Covenant of Grace to be born. It's the difference between worshiping a God of judgment or Abba, Daddy God whose Son Jesus died for our sins so we could be free.

From childhood I was set-up for performance-based relationships with those around me and with God. So, performance-based acceptance is another lifelong battle for me. I believe this comes from a woman's greatest fear—abandonment. Mine also comes from my need to be good enough. Unfortunately, my parents had made me feel inadequate and like I never measured up to their standards. Praise the Lord, he had a different idea! His grace makes us good enough. We just have to believe it.

Cal's middle-aged crazy and his Attention Deficit Disorder (undiagnosed, but we both acknowledged the symptoms) coupled with his job losses drove *me* crazy! He seemed to be what Thom Hartmann considers "a hunter" in *Attention Deficit Disorder: A Different Perspective*, while I'm "a farmer."[2]

Hunters are constantly prospecting and seeking opportunities to build new relationships, while farmers cultivate existing relationships. Cal couldn't stay still too long unless he was the center of attention (youngest child with A.D.D.). Life with Cal was sometimes like having traffic light moments: still for a few minutes and then off to the next thing or darting from one thing to another.

Being more of a farmer, I persevere until each task is completed. I tried to be as understanding as possible. The Lord helped to give me the strength and wisdom to deal with these differences. This is an example of one of the moments in our marriage where I had a chance to make important decisions about the attitude I would choose in my reaction toward Cal.

Don't forget that we can choose our attitudes. Sometimes, it's the only thing we can change. We can never change other people. We can only change ourselves.

Cal and I began to work closely to communicate our real feelings to one another. I think this is what made us a great couple. Open communication pertaining to feelings is the key.

Cal became considerate as I struggled to find my private, quiet place to study the Word and be alone with God. My office was too distracting for me and the nice little corner of our bedroom I set up for myself was hardly conducive when Cal was still in bed, asleep each morning. The Word and prayer have been the only solutions to keeping my priorities in balance. This was a spiritual battle the enemy and this world could have easily won had I not leaned so heavily on the Lord for support!

Cal recognized that he functioned more productively in a job with a boss to guide him. I didn't. That sometimes made me the bad guy when Cal had a bad day. My Sanguine strength in relationships was being applied to areas of business rather than to my relationship with Cal. I think he sometimes thought I wasn't there for him because of this.

I "make friends easily; am responsive to people; enjoyable and optimistic; always friendly and smiling; apologize easily; and converse with genuine warmth."[3] When Cal was hurting, no matter how I acted, my reactions just weren't right. This continually sparked my insecurity of not being good enough.

Admittedly, there were times when Cal didn't feel like a friend, when he was unresponsive to me. Then I didn't feel like being friendly and smiling, because I felt that he was the one who should apologize and that he didn't deserve my warmth.

It became a vicious cycle! Looking back and with the help of our youngest child, Tim who introduced me to *The Five Love Languages* by Gary Chapman, I can easily reflect on what was occurring. Since I didn't respect Cal, I wasn't providing him his love language of affirmation. This made him feel unloved and he stopped touching me (my love language).

That's when my own hurt surfaced. As strong as I was, I needed the reassurance of a strong husband that everything was going to be alright. And in his good times, Cal was fantastic at doing that. He could be so encouraging to our friends when they were going through challenging times. He always had such a warm, counseling heart. With all my heart I wanted him to take his rightful place as the head of our household. So, I'd pray, "Please, God, please!"

In *The Spirit Controlled Woman*, Barbara LaHaye recommends praying for "God to fill you with love for your husband so that you could genuinely love him regardless of your differences or his weaknesses."[4] Praise God, these prayers were being answered, even as Cal and I entered the difficult years of growing old together with the changes that brought.

What a responsibility! As the head of the family, the man is the provider.[5]

As I released hold of my life to God, Cal slowly began taking his rightful place as head and provider. Things got so much better. It was all in my attitude—giving my self to God and lifting Cal up in prayer—that created the transformation both of us needed. God was toppling another god in my life—the god of control. As God led me to release my idols, he brought me freedom. These changes were setting both Cal and I free. God's desire for believers is to have an abundant life, through Jesus.

I learned more about how destructive control can be when we lost my mother and I became closer to my dad and brother. Unfortunately, the control my mother attempted to use in her life (and my brother's dating life) was destructive in so many ways. Our kids and grandkids never had much of a chance to know my family. My brother has never married. Our mother had clearly been a stumbling block for my brother and dad's closeness to our family. I think we all felt the difference when she died. Even my Father God image was affected by my earthly father's weak image fostered by my mother's dominance and, perhaps, my father's mother's dominance too. The biblical image of wife was clearly affected by my mother's controlling actions toward my father.

I had to remember to pray, "Lord, let me see you as the strong Father I didn't have growing up. I have the loving part down, but not the strength of male dominance to keep this female relative of Eve in her place! I can do nothing in my own strength. It is all you, Lord. Holy Spirit guide me to be who you want me to be and show me how to stop relying on myself and to rely on you, who have proven yourself time after time!"

Early in my salvation and journey to learn how to yield to Cal I tried to share that concept with my mother (a believer), but she never seemed to hear me.

It wasn't until after her death, in one of my moments of missing her, that I reflected on reading materials she had by her chair about the difference between strong women versus women of strength.

> "A strong woman works out every day,
> Pride in her appearance she portrays,
> But a woman of strength kneels to pray,
> Her soul in shape, God leading the way."[6]

Apparently my mom had been a changing woman, just like me! She seemed to be working toward allowing the Lord to change her heart to a place of greater dependence upon him, instead of relying on herself.

I saw how much my dad needed her strength. Maybe she'd finally found the balance.

This was an encouragement to me and something I could share with Julie. Hopefully, she learned this lesson earlier in life than either my mother or I did when God reached down to guide us. I hoped she would be able to process this for herself even before she married. It could help her avoid this painful struggle for control and power within her own marriage.

This was such a commonsense approach for difficult times. I loved Cal, but when I prayed that God would help me to love him, I became more aware of it and at our next crisis I seemed to become less me-filled and more Spirit-filled! I'd pray, "Lord, you know that you are the only one who can get me through this and keep our marriage strong!"[7]

Was I just as sinful as everyone else? My own job losses became opportunities to create a final breaking point in my life. (I begged God to make me wiser each time!) Ever so slowly he showed me how to genuinely lean upon him and fully trust him!

God revealed to me that I had been using my work to cover up the things that were wrong, rather than going to him for his strength and direction. I desperately wanted my life experiences to count for something! I wanted to change, so I could make a real difference in our lives and in the lives of others.

For years I would pray "Oh, please, dear God, please! Make me into the woman of God you desire me to be!" I am finally seeing some real progress, but only at specific times. There is always such a long way to go!

I needed to search with God for answers. I certainly was hurt as a child by not being good enough. And this caused me to feel shame.

"Shame ... haunts us, nipping at our heels, feeding our deepest fear that we will end up abandoned and alone."[8]

I wasn't into the victim mentality at all. After all, I am a survivor! However, God does not call us just to be survivors. He calls us to live. Through the sacrifice made by Jesus, we are given life. If we are given life, then we are to live! Unlike the world, which is in survivor-mode, believers are called to live.

I had avoided all of this up to that point because my own business had satisfied me by putting me in a rewarding position of acceptance. I avoided the fear of abandonment due to not being good enough by making sure my achievements were much better than just good enough. My clients loved what I did for them and my self-worth was found through my business instead of through God. In most of my positions, I continued to attempt to over compensate in order to avoid judgment. All this avoidance, in reality, is from a survivor mentality. I wasn't seeing myself through God's eyes. I needed to explore this more. Clearly the Lord *had* made many of my work/career positions places of misery instead of shelter. He had been blocking my career path in an attempt to create a thirst for him within me. I could finally see that!

Eldredge's book pointed out Scriptures in Hosea just as I was in need of them. (Our Lord is always there for us, if we only stop and take time to search for him.)

> "Therefore I will block her path with thornbushes; I will wall her in so that she cannot find her way. She will chase after her lovers but not catch them; she will look for them but not find them. Then she will say, 'I will go back to my

husband as at first, for then I was better off than now.'" (Hosea 2:6–7)

That passage had so much significance for me! Not because of sexual infidelity, but because my workplace had become a path of thornbushes and I had neglected Cal (and the Lord) in so many ways. The Lord was speaking directly to my situation at the time and was calling me back to himself. In love, he had to block attempts until I turned to him and him alone for my rescue.

> "Therefore I am now going to allure her; I will lead her into the wilderness and speak tenderly to her." (Hosea 2:14)

I no longer feel like I did back then. I had felt like I was lost in a desert. Contrastingly, the desert can be a place of rest and very quiet.

We experienced this on a trip to Arizona. Cal and I stopped the car and we could actually "hear" the silence. I must continually find a desert within busy, noisy, bustling Orange County so I can reconnect with the Lord! The Word speaks of that reconnection.

> "'In that day,' declares the Lord, 'you will call me "my husband"; you will no longer call me "my master." …I will betroth you to me forever; I will betroth you in righteousness and justice, in love and compassion. I will betroth you in faithfulness, and you will acknowledge the Lord." (Hosea 2:16, 19–20)

God was calling me to be his beloved bride. I pleaded with God to show me where to go from there! I wanted to find his rest. I wanted to live. I was tired of being a survivor. The struggle was no longer mine. I gave it to him.

As I took more time to rest in the Lord, He gave me much encouragement and many more answers through his Word.

> "Unless the Lord builds the house, the builders labor in vain. Unless the Lord watches over the city, the guards stand watch in vain. In vain you rise early and stay up late, toiling for food to eat—for he grants sleep to those he loves." (Psalm 127:1–2)

> "For he will command his angels concerning you to guard you in all your ways; they will lift you up in their hands, so that you will not strike your foot against a stone. You will tread upon the lion and the cobra; you will trample the great lion and the serpent. 'Because he loves me,' says the Lord, 'I will rescue him; I will protect him, for he acknowledges my name. He will call upon me, and I will answer him; I will be with him in trouble, I will deliver him and honor him. With long life will I satisfy him and show him my salvation.'" (Psalm 91:11–16)

> "May the God of hope fill you with all joy and peace as you trust in him, so that you may overflow with hope by the power of the Holy Spirit." (Romans 15:13)

> "And my God will meet all your needs according to the riches of his glory in Christ Jesus." (Philippians 4:19)

> "The Lord foils the plans of the nations; he thwarts the purposes of the peoples. But the plans of the Lord stand firm forever, the purposes of his heart through all generations. Blessed is the nation whose God is the Lord, the people he chose for his inheritance. From heaven the Lord

looks down and sees all mankind; from his dwelling place he watches all who live on earth—he who forms the hearts of all, who considers everything they do." (Psalm 33:10-15)

I received so many encouragements and promises. I just needed to trust, follow his path, deal with forgiveness of my past, gain instruction in the way he had chosen for me, and believe this prosperity promise—seeing my hope in him.

I love how God's Word spoke directly to me in times of need. It reminded me of exactly what I was experiencing at the time. More importantly, I was reminded of God's love and protection for me as I did his will in my life. But there was always more work for me to do to commit to serving God instead of my self.

Therefore, in an effort to move to a place of even greater obedience, to find my rightful place as a woman of God, and to create balanced priorities for my life I could no longer avoid the dreaded Proverbs 31 Woman.

Chapter Wrap-Up:

Scriptures to consider:

> "Keep your lives free from the love of money and be content with what you have, because God has said, 'Never will I leave you; never will I forsake you.' So, we say with confidence, 'The Lord is my helper; I will not be afraid. What can mere mortals do to me?'" (Hebrews 13:5-6)

> "But godliness with contentment is great gain." (1 Timothy 6:6)

Are you content with where you are in life? If not, why not?

How do you relate to your spouse or significant other during tough times?

How are you grace-based or performance-based? How might that affect your relationships?

Do you make time for quiet time alone with God? When?

What idols in your life are replacing God's place in your life and/or the life of your family? (Don't forget about materialism, stuff, self-esteem in the eyes of the world or self-indulgence things like drugs, alcohol or food. Anything we lust after.)

Chapter 28

The Proverbs 31 Woman ...
Not Impossible with God

The Proverbs 31 Woman – A Worthy Woman

"An excellent woman [one who is spiritual, capable, intelligent, and virtuous], who is he who can find her?
Her value is more precious than jewels *and* her worth is far above rubies *or* pearls.

The heart of her husband trusts in her [with secure confidence],
And he will have no lack of gain.

She comforts, encourages, *and* does him only good and not evil.
All the days of her life.

She looks for wool and flax
And works with willing hands in delight.

She is like the merchant ships [abounding with treasure];
She brings her [household's] food from far away.

She rises also while it is still night.
And gives food to her household.
And assigns tasks to her maids.

She considers a field before she buys *or* accepts it [expanding her business prudently];
With her profits she plants fruitful vines in her vineyard.

She equips herself with strength [spiritual, mental, and physical fitness for her God-given task]
And makes her arms strong.

She sees that her gain is good;
Her lamp does not go out, but it burns continually through the night [she is prepared for whatever lies ahead].

She stretches out her hands to the distaff,
And her hands hold the spindle [as she spins wool into thread for clothing].

She opens *and* extends her hand to the poor,
And she reaches out her filled hands to the needy.

She does not fear the snow for her household,
For all in her household are clothed in [expensive] scarlet [wool].

She makes for herself coverlets, cushions, *and* rugs of tapestry.
Her clothing is linen, pure *and* fine, and purple [wool].

Her husband is known in the [city's] gates,
When he sits among the elders of the land.

She makes [fine] linen garments and sells them;
And supplies sashes to the merchants.

Strength and dignity are her clothing *and* her position is strong and secure;
And she smiles at the future [knowing that she and her family are prepared].

She opens her mouth in [skillful and godly] wisdom,
And the teaching of kindness is on her tongue [giving counsel and instruction].

She looks well to how things go in her household,
And does not eat the bread of idleness.

Her children rise up and call her blessed (happy, prosperous, to be admired);
Her husband also, and he praises her, *saying,*

"Many daughters have done nobly, *and* well [with the strength of character that is steadfast in goodness],
But you excel them all."

Charm *and* grace are deceptive, and [superficial] beauty is vain,
But a woman who fears the LORD [reverently worshiping, obeying, serving, and trusting him with awe-filled respect], she shall be praised.

Give her of the product of her hands,
And let her own works praise her in the gates [of the city]."
(Proverbs 31:10–31 AMP)

With much prayer and trepidation, I not only opened the Word to the Proverbs 31 Woman, but I investigated the response others have had to the role model she presents. Many scholars see the Proverbs 31 Woman as an example of positive attributes of a godly woman rather than an impossible standard to live up to all-in-one woman. It should be noted that this was what the mother of King Lemuel taught him. Therefore, we can't expect to be as prosperous or wealthy as this example of the perfect woman is. But there is good advice for all woman contained in the Proverbs 31.

Elsa Houtz, author of *The Working Mother's Guide to Sanity*, chose to translate the attributes of the Proverbs 31 into terms that today's busy working mother can understand.

She is a commendable wife and mother.

She lives for her home and family.

She is constantly industrious. This seemed like a very tiring thing to do—even for me!

She acts instead of worrying about the future.

She is self-disciplined and orderly.

She is a sharp businesswoman. I wondered how she got the money to buy the land. Perhaps she had a home-based business. I was homebased in business for years and my daughter-in-law, Heather and other son, Tim, work from home. Julie and Michael do their work from their home offices too. Now, in retirement, I enjoy my home office again.

She has good, refined taste.

She chooses her words carefully.

She demonstrates hospitality.

She is charitable in time of need. She remembers others in need. In retirement, I am now blessed through our frugal living to be able to donate more freely to those in need. I was drawn to the homeless who congregated at the Starbucks near one of my jobs. I used to give them food coupons to help them out. It feels really good to do what Jesus wants me to do. Thank you, Lord, for opening these doors and allowing me to be the giving person I was created to be.

She is virtuous because she is spiritually minded.

She is a woman worthy of respect. Her children praise her.[1] The Proverbs 31 Woman's children were obviously grown. Respect is a learned response—learned with age and maturity.

Gary Thomas in his book *Sacred Influence*, reminded me that "According to 1 Timothy 3:11, a man's qualification for spiritual office includes being married to a woman 'worthy of respect.'"[2]

Houtz adds, "The working mother is truly a treasure. She is more precious than the most valuable gems."[3]

A woman who knows the will of God and follows it is truly a woman of wisdom, one from whom we may all learn. She gains wisdom through fellowship with other believers, her daily study of the Word and praying—her communion with God.

I believe mothers following the example of the Proverbs 31 Woman will have children who become leaders in their communities. I believe this strongly. Well-raised children who become followers of Christ will become the leaders of tomorrow.

Wow! After all the study I've done about this Proverbs 31 Woman, could it possibly be that I have tried to emulate her because it was so easy for me to do? My personality characteristics certainly would seem to make it easier for me to be her. Yet another area to explore further with you, Lord!

But I believe the Proverbs 31 Woman is simply a guideline for us to strive toward to become the best wives and mothers that we can.

As I wrap this up, I clearly see my goal to be a Christ-follower requires that I be completely sold-out in my relationship to Jesus. I need to worship God only and not leave any room in my heart for all the other stuff that takes me away and distracts me from him. I pray often, "Lord, continue to help me surrender *all* to you and *fully* trust you!"

I praise God for motivating me to better my own marriage to Cal so I could become an example for other wives and wives-to-be. I am thankful for the wisdom God provided in his Word and the words of others sent to guide me. I wish you all the best in improving your marriage as you learn to love your own husbands even better.

Chapter Wrap-Up:

Does the Proverbs 31 Woman leave you feeling pressured or relieved?

What things are you doing well?

In what areas could you use improvement?

How does this book inspire you to make changes in your marriage and/or how you relate to one another?

Conclusion

Love After Loss?

As a widow, I began forging a future by myself.

I finally settled into the single, widowed life and for a little over a year had begun enjoying my "freedom." (Certainly, that's not to say I felt tied down with Cal in any way, but the last few years of his life had restricted our activities.) I had just discovered a new, freer lifestyle and things were going ahead pretty smoothly when the COVID-19 pandemic hit the world!

Only a few months at home passed before the isolation got to me. I started investigating websites for singles and found an opportunity to go to a Christian singles' camping weekend. I love to camp, but Cal wasn't much of a camper so I welcomed the opportunity to safely go camping despite concerns about COVID-19.

The trip wasn't what I expected, but it was fun. Like those old junior high dances, with girls on one side and guys on the other, the structure of the weekend limited opportunities to get to know other men as dating partners. Of course, I was probably the oldest one there and didn't want to date anyone close to my kids' ages either. But there were really good speakers and the worship music was awesome. The focus was more on divorced singles. I think there were only a couple of us widows.

Following the campout, I began to explore online dating under the tutelage of Julie who had dated until she was around forty. I call her my dating coach!

With her encouragement and guidance, I tried online dating, but found it very frustrating. Many of the men seemed only to want to text. When I finally got them to video chat with me, I had to take all kinds of measures to conceal my identity. (I was building a side hustle and have an unusual last name.)

I longed for an opportunity to meet single men face-to-face, which I felt was the best way to get to know each other. But COVID-19 caused many to be fearful and in-person meetups were difficult to arrange.

I finally decided the whole dating thing was just too much work and I was fine right where I was, though I did miss just simple male companionship. Cal had been such a wonderful best friend, adding a male perspective on life, and I missed that component.

Off and on I would check out online dating sites and meetup events. Eventually, I did find a Christian man who was comfortable doing a video chat. He even came up for lunch outside on a patio to meet in person.

He was nice but, honestly, I wasn't attracted to him so much. He was the first date I'd had since I was seventeen!

Julie encouraged me to give him one more chance, so he came up again to take me out to a COVID-19-safe parking lot dinner. A few things signaled to me that we just weren't a match, but then—and I give him an amazing amount of credit for telling me this—he shared he'd been sent to prison for manslaughter with the use of a gun as a young man.

Oh, my!

I certainly believe in forgiveness, but this freaked me out. I was now on a scary date! This was the first time I'd dated since I was in high school and I felt afraid.

I prayed for a gracious way to "make my escape"! Later, I sent him a text similar to one Julie had used during her dating career.

I was as caring as I could be, saying that I didn't want to be in the way of his finding someone with whom he might be more compatible. But there was just something missing and I didn't want to hold him back from finding a loving, perfect relationship.

Well, it took me a while to recover from that online dating experience to say the least!

I settled back into my comfortable routine and decided being a single widow was just fine for now.

A few months later I found a meetup event that looked interesting. Virtual Speed Dating eliminated the stupid texting and emailing back and forth of online dating and cut to the chase. The idea was that several male and female singles were led by a facilitator who sent them into breakout rooms for a few minutes, one-on-one, to see if there were any sparks that might ignite.

I decided I'd give this one more chance and I signed up. I could see the possibilities, although it took a couple of meetings to find someone compatible with my beliefs.

One attractive man was also interested in me. I liked the fact that he was a sixty-year-old man who had returned to college to get his degree. I might avoid the pain of an early death with a man significantly younger than myself. Maybe he'd even outlive me. He was very different from me and I was intrigued to find out more. We met for coffee outside on a patio just before Christmas.

A few days later he asked me out for New Year's (COVID-19 style). He drove down to meet me so we could walk in the local harbor and enjoy the Christmas lights. We had pizza and each returned to our separate homes to see the New Year come in together on FaceTime. If getting COVID-19 wasn't a concern, I would have kissed him before we parted. I liked him a lot.

He called me every night to say good night, but whenever I asked him important faith questions, he would dodge the subject, only saying his grandmother had taken him to church faithfully as a child. But I needed more. I was also concerned he really didn't have the time for me in his life. I didn't want to push that, of course, because my goal was to support him in any way I could so he could fulfill his dream of a college education.

I pushed for one more date in person, so we could learn a bit more about each other. Following that date, I knew I had to break it off because he wasn't a committed Christian and I was really attracted to him. He also seemed to have other motives for the relationship and I saw no future in continuing.

For him, I couldn't just send him the breakup text, so I called him and broke it off. As nervous as I was to make the call, I know I did the right thing telling him how important my faith was to me and that I just couldn't see us moving forward.

How glad I am that I moved on and that I hadn't kissed my New Year's date that year. That meant that my first kiss with anyone other than my precious Cal could be saved for someone special.

About four months later I noticed a meetup group for widowed persons that was having an in-person meeting.

The isolation of COVID-19 and my gregarious, people-loving personality drove me to want to try it out. I did sneak a look at the men who were going to attend and one stood out. His profile said he liked hiking and camping—a bonus for me. He played guitar. He was an avid reader and sounded smart about things I'd love to know more about.

He sounded lonely, looking for a friend. I knew I could be a friend. He was also semi-retired with his own business, so he seemed perfect. I hoped he could understand my entrepreneurial bent and forgive my workaholic tendencies. And he was sooo handsome that I had to sign up to go.

I had returned to work and wasn't sure how long it would take me to get to the meeting, so I arrived early and figured I would sit at the bar until the meeting started. However, the hostess indicated one person was already there. I had difficulty holding back my enthusiasm when I recognized the good-looking guy sitting in front of me was the man with whom I seemed to have so much in common.

We had about an hour alone before the rest of the (mostly women) arrived.

When I got up to leave that night, he asked if he could call me and I rapidly responded, "Absolutely!"

We had a traditional first-date dinner on the local pier followed by a hike overlooking the ocean for our second date.

Between those two dates I had much to contemplate. We each shared more about the lost loves of our lives. As he shared more about his beloved wife and her sudden death, I was touched by the prophetic words she had said to him.

"Honey," she'd said, "I want you to know that if anything ever happens to me, you have my permission to find someone. We both know that you will be miserable alone."

He told me he questioned her immediately.

"Are you feeling ill? I'm eight years older than you and have already had a heart attack and a stroke. It is not going to be you. I'm the walking time bomb!"

She replied, "I just don't want you to be alone. I love you."

The following year she collapsed at her desk at work from a brain aneurysm rupture. She died five weeks later.

His recount of this reminded me of how the Lord God said, "It is not good (beneficial) for the man to be alone; I will make him a helper [one who balances him—a counterpart who is] suitable *and* complementary for him." (Genesis 2:18 AMP)

As I heard more about the sudden loss of his precious wife of thirty years, I vowed to tread carefully with his wounded heart.

On our first date, he shared that I was the first person he had dated since her death three years before. I took this heavy responsibility seriously and analyzed how I really felt about him, especially when he expressed concern over how I felt about him having similar health issues to Cal's.

Though it was hard to think of that in the moment, I was determined to see if our personalities, interests, and attraction to one another was genuine and could last.

He had a very good point about his health issues, especially in light of my desire to control all that with looking for a man ten years younger. But I'm not in control. God is and he brought us together.

Our adventures continued and I found this man was growing on me! I was beginning to see the sweet, caring, spiritual heart within this man and I slowly accepted that I would see this through.

I'm glad I chose to persevere! We both had amazingly crazy, quirky personalities. He got me! My nutty sense of humor came out of the shadows. To have another adult appreciate my personality and get my warped sense of humor was so refreshing!

Though we didn't really know how to "date," we enjoyed each other's company and became good friends who fell in love. We went to church, dinner, and on hikes together. We watched sci-fi movies together, went antiquing, volunteered together at the gallery where his photos hang, and met each other's kids and grandkids.

I was blessed to help him grow in his relationship with Jesus too. He appreciated the time we spent at The Shoreline Church of San Clemente and at our Wednesday night Life Group.

Kirk reignited his love for Jesus in his search for a new understanding of the faith of his youth. I showed him that God cares about even the smallest most mundane things in our lives.

I remember one day we were looking for a parking space in Laguna Beach and I just prayed out loud for God to find us a space and Kirk was amazed when we got the perfect spot!

Cal and I had a full and, in so many ways, complete life. I began to feel I could have that with Kirk too as we started journeying through this old age thing together.

Little did I know I would lose Kirk exactly three years to the day that I lost Cal. In the hospital, Kirk died of an infection while waiting to have heart surgery. He was in my life for only eight months and sixteen days, but I regret nothing of the love we both found during our time together.

The deaths of both Cal and then, Kirk, caused life storms for me, but Jesus is my living hope and he meets me wherever I am. I am not alone.

Chapter Wrap-Up:

Who do you know who might be afraid to try love again?

What ways could you help them step out of their shell?

Acknowledgments

To Chris Brown, who helped me along my early journey and, more importantly, encouraged me to write everything down. Now I have the story! Thank you, Chris.

To Jim Alessi, whose encouragement as a fellow Christian helped me take the most important step of my life.

To Angie Strada, who dared to share her transformation with me and those many other saints—faces without names … thank you all so much!

To Jody Bucknam, Suzanne Elliot, and Carolyn O'Campo, who listened to me and listened to me and listened to me, ad nauseam! Thank you for your caring patience!

To young mom and new friend, Tammy Porter who is helping me grow in new directions to understand God better.

To the many pastors and teachers who have been in the right place at the right time by God's perfect design. You are far too many to mention individually, but my thanks go out to all of you.

To my special prayer partner, Jackie Newby, who has listened, shared, and prayed me through my early trials.

To my accountability partner, Janet McCurdy, who saw me from a fresh perspective, yet was able to warn me when I slipped into old patterns.

Finally, to the two young women closest to me, our daughter, Julie and Todd's wife, Heather, as they have become wonderful wives and mothers.

About the Author

Author and Keynote Speaker, Jeanne Gormick, has been a college instructor, a member of MOPS Speaker Network, owned a Public Relations firm and was the Vice President of a home care company among other positions within the senior industry, is a mom, grammy, and has won numerous awards. But her greatest achievement was her almost 50-year marriage to her beloved late husband Cal.

Now a widow, Jeanne strives to inspire, encourage, and engage newlyweds or those thinking of getting married to create a treasured marriage and long-lasting love with God's help. Her upbeat and spunky personality brings fun to any conversation!

Endnotes

Chapter 6

1. *The Family: God's Masterpiece,* Helen Duff Baugh, Thomas Nelson Publishers, Nashville, TN, 1994, 28.

2. *Faith That Follows: Experiencing Discipleship to Jesus,* Seth Ebel, The Shoreline Church of San Clemente, San Clemente, CA, 2012, 25.

Chapter 8

1. *Captivating: Unveiling the Mystery of a Woman's Soul,* John and Stasi Eldredge, Thomas Nelson Publishers, Nashville, TN, 2007, 41.

Chapter 9

1. Thomas, 221.

2. *The Confident Woman: Knowing Who You Are in Christ,* Anabel Gillham, Harvest House Publishers, Eugene, OR, 1993, 167.

3. *Woman—Aware and Choosing,* Betty J. Coble, Broadman Press, Nashville, TN, 1975, 31, 62.

4. Ebel, 113.

5. *Creative Counterpart: Becoming the Woman, Wife, and Mother You Have Longed To Be,* Linda Dillow, Thomas Nelson Publishers, Nashville, TN, 1975, 103–120.

6. Thomas, 23.

7. Coble, 63.

8. Ebel, 22.

9. Thomas, 65.

10. Ibid, 32.

11. Ibid, 56.

12. Ibid, 61.

13. Ibid, 36, 40.

14. Coble, 59, 64.

15. *Emotionally Healthy Spirituality Day by Day: A 40-Day Journey with the Daily Office,* Peter Scazzero, Zondervan, Grand Rapids, MI, 2018, 79.

Chapter 10

1. *Fatherless America: Confronting Our Most Urgent Social Problem,* David Blankenhorn, Harper Perennial, New York, NY, 1996.

2. *Total Truth: Liberating Christianity from Its Cultural Captivity,* Nancy Pearcey, Crossway, Wheaton, IL, 2005, 346, 347.

3. Coble, 102.

4. Ibid, 104.

5. Dillow, 43–66

6. Thomas, 92.

Chapter 11

1. The Message of Ephesians (The Bible Speaks Today Series), John Stott. From A Commentary 1/22/17. *Used by permission of Inter-Varsity Press UK, Nottingham. All rights reserved.*

2. Coble, 38–39.

Chapter 12

1. Thomas, 112.

2. Ibid, 49.

Chapter 13

1. Dillow, back cover.

2. Smith, Lynn. "A Dream Denied: They Wanted It All," *LA Times,* October 12, 1994, https://www.latimes.com/archives/la-xpm-1994-10-12-ls-49456-story.html

3. Thomas, 232.

4. *Intentional Faith: Aligning Your Life with the Heart of God,* Allen Jackson, Thomas Nelson Publishers, Nashville, TN, 2020, 85.

5. Ibid, 82.

Chapter 14

    1. Thomas, 62.

    2. Ibid, 79.

    3. Ibid, 80.

    4. Ibid, 75.

Chapter 16

    1. Shabsigh, Dr. Ridwan. "Testosterone Deficiency: Testing and Treatments," accessed March 14, 2022, https://www.drridwan.com/urology-health-issues/testosterone-deficiency-treatment.php.

    2. Thirumavalavan, Nannan, Wilken, Nathan A, Ramasamy, Ranjith. "Hypogonadism and renal failure: An update," accessed March 14, 2022, https://pubmed.ncbi.nlm.nih.gov/25878406/.

Chapter 17

    1. Coble, 39.

Chapter 19

    1. *Sacred Influence*, Gary Thomas, Zondervan, Grand Rapids, MI, 2006, 235.

Chapter 21

    1. *The Birth Order Book*, Dr. Kevin Leman, Fleming H. Revell Company, Old Tappan, NJ, 1984, 177.

    2. Ibid, 84.

    3. Ibid, 11.

Chapter 22

1. Smalley, Gary. "Gary Smalley Personality Types Inventory," accessed March 17, 2022, https://www3.dbu.edu/jeanhumphreys/SocialPsych/smalleytrentpersonality.htm.

Chapter 23

1. *The Spirit Controlled Woman*, Beverly LaHaye, Harvest House Publishers, Eugene, OR, 1995, 68.

2. Ibid, 71.

3. Ibid, 74.

4. Ibid, 81–85.

5. Ibid, 20.

6. Ibid, 114.

Chapter 24

1. *How We Love*, Milan & Kay Yerkovich, WaterBook Press, Colorado Springs, CO, 2006, 6.

2. Ibid, 7.

3. Ibid, 17.

4. Ibid, 49.

5. Ibid, 50.

6. Ibid, 123, 125.

7. Ibid, 50.

Chapter 25

1. Thomas, 104.

2. Ibid.

3. *Men Are From Mars Women Are From Venus,* John Gray, PhD, Harper Collins, New York, NY, 1992, 26.

4. Ibid, 157.

5. Ibid.

Chapter 27

1. Eldredge, 50–52.

2. *Attention Deficit Disorder: A Different Perspective,* Thom Hartmann, Underwood Books, San Francisco, CA, 1997, 24–27.

3. LaHaye, 85.

4. Ibid, 160–161.

5. Baugh, 19.

6. Hunter, Luke. "A Strong Woman Vs. A Woman Of Strength Poem," Poemhunter.com, September 20, 2006, https://www3.dbu.edu/jeanhumphreys/SocialPsych/smalleytrentpersonality.htm.

7. LaHaye, 167.

8. Eldredge, 7.

Chapter 28

1. *The Working Mother's Guide to Sanity*, Elsa Houtz, Harvest House Publishing, Irving, CA, 1989, 136–139.

2. Thomas, 22.

3. Houtz, 135.

Further Reading

Attention Deficit Disorder: A Different Perspective, Thom Hartmann, Underwood Books, Grass Valley, CA, 1993. (189 pgs.)

Creative Counterpart, Linda Dillow, Thomas Nelson Publishers, Nashville, TN, 1975. (168 pgs.)

Emotionally Healthy Spirituality Day by Day, Peter Scazzero, Zondervan, Grand Rapids, MI 2018. (194 pgs.)

Faith That Follows Experiencing Discipleship in Jesus, Seth Ebel, The Shoreline Church of San Clemente, San Clemente, CA, 2012. (113 pgs.)

Fatherless America: Confronting Our Most Urgent Social Problems, David Blankenhorn, Basic Books, New York, 1995. (328 pgs.)

How We Love, Milan & Kay Yerkovich, WaterBook Press, Colorado Springs, CO, 2006. (305 pgs.)

Intentional Faith Aligning Your Life with the Heart of God, Allen Jackson, Nelson Books, Nashville, TN, 2020. (222 pgs.)

Men Are From Mars Women Are From Venus, John Gray, PhD, Harper Collins, New York, NY 1992. (286 pgs.)

Sacred Influence by Gary Thomas, Zondervan, Grand Rapids, Michigan 2006. (262 pgs.)

The Birth Order Book, Dr. Kevin Leman, Fleming H. Revell Company, Old Tappan, New Jersey. 1985 (190 pgs.)

The Confident Woman, Anabel Gillham, Harvest House Publishers, Eugene, OR, 1993 (273 pgs.)

The Five Love Languages: How to Express Heartfelt Commitment to Your Mate, Gary Chapman, Northfield Publishing, Chicago, IL 1995. (204 pgs.)

The Message of Ephesians: Being a Christian. The Bible Speaks Today, John Stott. From A Commentary 1/22/17. *Used by permission of Inter-Varsity Press UK, Nottingham. All rights reserved.)*

The Spirit Controlled Woman, Beverly LaHaye, Harvest House Publishers, Eugene, OR, 1995. (274 pgs.)

The Working Mother's Guide to Sanity, Elsa Houtz, Harvest House Publishers, Eugene, OR, 1989. (155 pgs.)

Total Truth Liberating Christianity from Its Cultural Captivity, Nancy Pearcey, Crossway, Wheaton, Illinois, 2005 (511 pgs.)

Woman—Aware and Choosing, Betty J. Coble, Broadman Press, Nashville, TN, 1975 (155 pgs.)